How to Get Your Wife to Sleep with Chicks

By Robert J. Eagle

How to Get Your Wife to Sleep With Chicks

ISBN: 978-1-4583-3822-8

For information on how to reproduce selections from this book, please contact permissions@BigManMedia.net.

 media

www.BigManMedia.net

Note: This book contains the opinions and ideas of its author. He is crazy. The book is sold with the understanding that the author and publisher are not engaged in rendering professional services or advice. This is intended for entertainment purposes only.

Table of Contents

Introduction 5
1: The Time Investment 9
2: Build Her Confidence 13
3: Language is Key 23
4: It's Give and Take 39
5: Finding the Right Woman...43
6: Seek the Wisdom of Others 53
7: Make a Move..59
   Pavlov's Dog...59
   The Smart Mouse Gets the Cheese............................61
   When in Rome… 64
   The Forbidden Fruit...65
   Paying Strangers to Help..65
   Hypnosis...66
   The Spokesman 68
   Phonetics 71
   Alcohol...73
   Pull the Trigger..75
8: Believe it Can Happen 77
Appendix A: Girl on Girl Videos....................................81
Appendix B: Things Chicks Dig 83
Appendix C: What Book Are You Reading?....................85

Introduction

First of all, the ideas contained in the following pages are not the result of an intensive university study conducted by leading psychologists around the world. You will not find any ancient Chinese secrets purporting the many uses of the Bengal Tiger's anatomy. What you are about to read is the result of many afternoons of shooting the shit with my friends, trying to get laid with two women at once. Some of us have been successful, and others have been remarkably adept at failure. This book, then, is a patchwork of the strategies, tactics, and objectives that have led us towards the accomplishment of our mission: to get our wives to sleep with chicks.

The idea for this book came about in during a road trip I took with my buddy. We were sharing stories of close encounters with the bi-sexual kind and the ways we inevitably squandered our opportunities. We shared our successes and failures and traded ideas... and then it dawned on us. Men should devise a way to pass on the information gained through their experiences to other men, so that we would not face the same failures over and over again. "We must do it for the greater good," I said, "the greater good."

Our first idea was to put a mark on each woman who we had discovered to have an interest in other women. It could be a branding of sorts, perhaps on the back of her neck hidden by her hair. This way, when a man met a woman for the first time, he could nonchalantly tassle her hair and inspect her neck for the mark.

The branding idea seemed to have a couple problems. We weren't sure how we would coordinate a worldwide effort among men to all use and recognize the same mark. We also couldn't ignore the fact that it would be incredibly difficult to burn a mark on a woman without her knowing that something was up.

We considered compiling an elaborate database of female ménage a trois participants and, presumably, we could store their names in the men's room of her home county's nearest highway rest stop. An attendant at the visitor center outside Eugene, Oregon tipped us off that, logistically speaking, it just wasn't realistic.

We eventually came to the idea of passing on the knowledge in a slightly more conspicuous fashion: publishing a book and advertising it in all the major bookstores worldwide. Fortunately, we realized that all the publicity such a book would generate could destroy all hope of success for which the book was intended. Unfortunately, we were already so used to the idea of making money on the venture that we had to write this, albeit with a smaller marketing budget and without the sign in front of Barnes and Noble.

Many people might argue that it is a futile battle to try and get your wife to sleep with other women. They argue that certain people are predisposed to those behaviors. I adamantly disagree. This debate has striking similarities to the questions raised by Plato and Aristotle. Are people born with certain skills, abilities, and personality, or do all of these develop as a result of experience? Are certain ideas and feelings innate, or are they learned?

More recently it has been the 17th century French philosopher René Descartes and the British philosophers Thomas Hobbes and John Locke debating the topic. The only reason I know any of this is because I took a philosophy class in college. I needed a three credit elective that met after 10 a.m. but before 3 p.m., and course content was really a secondary consideration. I am just grateful for the opportunity to toss their names around as if I remembered something about their theories.

Regardless, I can sum up all this philosophy jazz in one word: "vomit." Bisexual tendencies are not like recessive genes where you either have them or you don't. It is essentially like vomiting. People don't go around vomiting everyday, and yet anyone can vomit at any time simply by putting their finger down their throat. Similarly, all women have the potential for bi-sexuality. They simply need to be persuaded to stick their finger down their throat. And notice I said "persuaded." It's a fine line between persuasion and coercion, and it's important that you never get caught[1] on the wrong side of that line. Once you have convinced them to stick their finger down their throat it's your opportunity to be there when the full body heave starts.

Throughout the course of this book I will use the term wife, but you can interpret that to mean your wife, your girlfriend, your lover, or whatever else. Let me also say that there are many different partner permutations that one may find desirable beyond simply your woman having sex with another woman. Some men will be happy with their wives getting it on with another woman even though they do not get to participate. Other men are happy with two women screwing him but not pleasuring each other at all. There are a lot of ways that this pleasure cruise can set sail. You might be lucky enough to have a specific fantasy fulfilled, but I caution you to not be too rigid in your expectations or your requests. Much like the cockroach, adaptability is the key to survival.

Finally, before you begin reading this I need you to promise yourself two things. The importance of these promises can not be stressed enough. Your livelihood, your success, in fact, your very existence may depend on it. First, you must resolve to destroy this book immediately upon finishing it. You must leave no evidence that you ever had it, that you ever wanted it, that you were ever remotely interested in the idea of two women at once. The thought never fucking crossed your mind. Do not give the book to anyone else, because someone is liable to trace it back to you. Remember that Lifetime movie where the guy cheats on his wife and writes down the directions to the motel on a napkin and leaves them in his pants pocket? Then his wife finds it while doing the laundry and hires someone to kill him. Same thing here! Burn it, eat it—do whatever you have to do—just make sure no one finds it.

Even more important—DO NOT TAKE THIS TOO SERIOUSLY!!!! Do not take my word as gospel. If you are one

---

[1] Do what you have to do. Just don't get caught.

of those people that totally buys into everything that you read, let me draw your attention to the following legal disclaimer:

Robert J. Eagle and Big Man Media disclaim all responsibility for criminal behavior or civil liability incurred as a consequence of use and application of the contents of this book. Both parties do, however, reserve the right to sell the story to the producers of Law and Order and/or similar entertainment outlets in the event of litigation.

1: The Time Investment

Before you even begin to try and persuade your woman to sleep with other chicks, it is important that you understand that it is a long process. It could take a really, *really* long time.

I could write a bunch of garbage like, "good things come to those who wait" and other fortune cookie proverbs, but that's not the reality of it. Honestly, most of us daydream about something like this our whole pathetic lives, never doing anything about it, and we ultimately die bitter and unfulfilled. Then there are those of us who toil in the fields of lust trying to cultivate some sense of sexual adventure in our women, only to die just as bitter and unfulfilled after a life of failure.

Of course, there are a few lucky sons of bitches that fall ass-backwards into a lesbian colony and get chosen as the resident penis. I'm undecided on whether to hate these bastards or revere them. Today I'm leaning towards hating them, because when you talk to these guys you get the sense that they had absolutely nothing to do with arranging their threesome. It just happened to them. They came home early from work and heard voices in the bedroom, or they were out drinking and ended up getting two freebies at a brothel in Cleveland. It's just sick, because I've worked so damn hard and seen people I love work so damn hard. These guys are hitting the trifecta their first time to the racetrack without even reading a program. And the worst part of it is that they don't ever seem to appreciate it.

I've gotten off to a somewhat pessimistic start, but it is only to keep you from running up to your woman and blurting out something stupid without thinking. You can achieve your dreams. It does happen, and it happens to people like you if you are willing to work at it and dedicate your mind to the task. This is a delicate matter, not one that can be taken on whimsically or without a second thought. You cannot just pull her close to you in bed one night and say, "Honey, I'd really love it if we could get another woman over here to have sex with us." The lucky ones will get laughed at. The not so lucky ones will spend the night fighting and reassuring and ultimately sleeping on the couch for many nights to come. You have to work up to the point when you can seriously broach the subject without putting yourself in imminent danger and with a genuine chance of a positive response.

Did you ever hear that story about the frog in the boiling water? It goes something like this: if you place a frog in a pan of boiling hot water, he will immediately jump out and save himself, but if you place a frog in cool water and slowly heat the water to boiling, he will sit in the water and allow himself to be cooked. The frog doesn't notice subtle changes in his environment. He only notices the abrupt changes. Women are similar creatures. If you throw the idea of sleeping with chicks at your woman, she is bound to jump out of the pot and save herself. However, if you slowly heat the water and increase her tolerance for all things kinky, you can boil your frog in a big pot of love stew.

For most men I recommend a five-year plan. That applies to guys that have approached the subject in the past and were rebuffed. That applies to guys with women who have self-confidence issues. It also applies to those of you who are afraid of a violent backlash. Over this five-year period of time you will implement a variety of tactics and adhere to one or more strategies to achieve your main objective. You should see gradual, as opposed to abrupt changes in your woman. Perhaps she will begin to be more flirtatious in groups, she will remark to you when she sees an attractive woman, or maybe just allowing you to remark when you see an attractive woman will be a significant accomplishment.

Imagine being out on a date with your wife and you see an incredibly gorgeous woman at the bar. Your wife sees you staring at her ass, but rather than bitch you out she calmly gets up from your table, walks up to the woman and invites her over to your table. That's the stuff utopian societies are built upon. That's what we need to work towards. It's not about stricter gun laws or universal health coverage. This is the shit that makes a difference in your life.

What can be frustrating is that this project will take a seemingly enormous amount of time, and yet one moment of ignorance (or *arrogance*) will cost you any chance you ever had at a threesome. You should think of this as a chess match. And I don't mean those chess matches where the whiz kids move the pieces around like lightning and tap those clocks back and forth. I'm talking about how normal people play the game. We stare at the board for ten minutes moving things around without letting our hands leave the piece. We try and think back to that Bobby Fisher movie and recall what he did when he was playing Laurence Fishburne in the park. What the hell did he do when his queen was trapped by a horse and a little castle thing? We don't know how to play, we aren't sure of any of the moves we make, and we don't want the queen to kill the king. We play slow and cautious.

Likewise, we have only a vague idea of how to achieve our goal of the threesome and there just aren't enough good mainstream movies that deal with this subject. What do we have to work with? I'm racking my brain and going all the way back to Larry from Three's Company? How about every character ever played by Charlie Sheen? Or Sam Malone from Cheers? He was good, but very few of us are ex-pitchers who drive Corvettes.

> Give your plan a name. Give it some real character, like The Marshall Plan, The Manhattan Project or Southern Reconstruction.

For those of you who are ball players with fast cars, I suggest you trade this book for a quarter so that you can buy yourself a clue. You don't need this book, because the only advice I can give you and is the only advice you need. Show it off! There is no shame in flaunting your wealth, fame and athleticism. It may not win you lifelong friends, but instant sexual gratification beats friendship any day of the week.

I got off track, but the point was that most of us don't know what we are doing, we have no good role models, so we must proceed with caution.

Getting back to the plan, sometimes five years can be overkill. A three-year plan may be appropriate for those couples that already have a pretty daring sex life. For those women who are into having sex in public places, anal intercourse, toys, videos, etc., it isn't such a stretch for them to make it with a woman. With them, it all comes down to how you approach it. The minimum time period I could recommend is a twelve-month plan, which just accelerates the three-year plan. Anything less than one year and you are just pushing your luck. Rome was not built in a day, but eventually orgies were so common they named 'em after the city.

Before you get started, I think it's a good idea to give your plan a name. Give it some real character, like The Marshall Plan, The Manhattan Project or Southern Reconstruction. Then it has some purpose, some life, and you can refer to it with your buddies without your women being any the wiser. An acquaintance of mine in Maryland once told me that Operation Desert Fox[2] was actually the name of an Air Force General's plan to get his wife with one of the clerks at the Pentagon book store. Somehow a member of the media overheard him talking about it and assumed it was a military operation. Rather than abandon his scheme for satisfying sex, the General went along with it and recommended air strikes on Baghdad. Such commitment to a mission is so rare among civilians. We should all take note of this fine soldier's example.

---

[2] This was a brief skirmish in Iraq resulting from Saddam Hussein's invasion of Kuwait. The history of this raises the question, if it was okay to invade Iraq, wreck it and leave back in 1991, why hang around for so long the second time?

2: Build Her Confidence

Before a woman can allow her man to lay down with another, she must feel confident that she will not lose him to this new chick. In the first stage of your plan you must build this confidence, and you must do it steadily over time. It has to be done in such a way so as not to arouse suspicion. Women have these antennae that can sense when we are conniving. They are insatiable whiners when we pay them little attention, and they are trustless demons when you shower them with affection. They know when something is up so you must take care to hide your true motivations.

There is also the real possibility that if you provide too much affection or support early on in amounts that you cannot sustain over the long haul, she will resent you when you begin to scale back on those affections. This only undermines the work you will have done previously and leaves you further away from your ultimate goal.

For those people who want an overview of the kinds of things you're going to need to do I have provided a "DO LIST" and a "DO NOT DO LIST" with suggestions for building your woman's self-confidence.

#1

DO: Keep a note inside your shoe to remind yourself to tell your woman that she looks beautiful in the morning. If you can, find something specific each morning to make a positive comment about.

DO NOT: Say the same damn thing over and over again so that she knows you have put no thought whatsoever into your comments and you come across as insincere.

DO: Let her find the note in your shoe after a few weeks by asking her very politely to help you find your shoes. Make sure the shoes are in a place she will quickly find. When she finds the note and questions you, simply say, "Honey, it was just so important for me to make you feel good in the morning that I didn't want to take a chance that I might forget." Assuming that you have kept up with your morning compliments, this gem is worth like two dozen morning compliments. Use this when you really want to get laid that night.

DO NOT: Phrase the note "Tell the bitch something sweet" or something equally offensive. Such action will insure your celibacy for many moons.

#2

DO: Buy her flowers for no apparent reason.

DO NOT: Screw anything up for the three days prior or the four days after the flowers are given. There must be no perceived connection between the flowers and the shit you pulled.

DO: Deliver the flowers in a creative way. I once left the bouquet on the kitchen counter right where my woman would see them when she first woke up. She loved it and she still talks about it (probably because that was like the only time she ever got flowers). You can probably find more romantic ways to do it in one of those magazines that they read, but that's the best I've got.

DO NOT: Get the cheapest damn flowers available. Go to a real florist. Do not buy them at the gas station.

#3

DO: Rent a limo for the night, get all dressed up and take her to some classy event like the opera, a musical, or an ice skating show.

DO NOT: Bitch through the whole show about how the guy skaters are gay or how the songs in the musical all sound like the same crap from "The Sound of Music."

DO: Watch the movie *Titanic* if you need to learn how to behave like a gentleman when you're out with classy people. That scrub guy who dies at the end doesn't really know anything either, but I thought he handled himself well.

DO NOT: Turn the movie off after you have studied all the relevant mannerisms in *Titanic*. All you really need to see is in the first ninety minutes, but leave it on for her to watch the next four hours. Chicks think it's romantic or something. Also, do not ruin the ending for her. Sometimes they believe that if Kate and Leo love each other enough then the boat won't sink.

DO: Try and get her to have sex with you in the limo. That is so cool!

Try out some of these dos and don'ts and think of some of your own as well. When brainstorming just think of a really cool guy who was good with women and do what he would do. Then think of a complete loser and don't do what he would do. Got it?

Now, my "Do guy" is Vince Vaughn's character from *Wedding Crashers*. He was dedicated to his craft, regimented in his approach and nailed a bunch of hot women. He learned all that he could from his mentor, Chaz[3], and then took what he learned and melded it with his own style. I might see a chick on the street that would look good in bed with me and my wife, but she's not wearing red hooker pumps. My instinct might be to let her walk on by, but then I remember Rule #76: *No excuses. Play like a champion!*

Some additional "Do Guys" might be Paul Rudd, pick any George Clooney character, or Peyton Manning. I don't dig the Colts, but the man knows how to execute. This is personal—pick a guy that fits your style.

I have a hundred "Don't Guys." Bob Saget, Napoleon Dynamite, Anakin Skywalker, and Steve Bartman[4] top my list. If you are riding public transportation while reading this, look to your left and you'll probably find five more. There are another half dozen working in your office right now.

One of the things that I do to try and raise my wife's level of acceptance of my natural male tendencies is to tell her how far she has already come. After complimenting her, I think she herself wants to improve on it. When my wife and I were first married, I couldn't look at another woman's face without her

---

[3] Will Ferrell is fantastic as Chaz. That first scene of his with the nunchucks and the meatloaf is absolutely hysterical.

[4] Chicago Cubs fans know who this is. The rest of you can stop looking at me while I'm crying.

pulling this pouty little girl act on me. I started complimenting her on how far she has progressed in accepting my reactions to chicks with nice tits[5]. The truth is she really wasn't where I wanted her to be, but she had made significant strides. After my compliment I think she took pride in not giving me hell when I glanced at a chick's ass. Now she will even compliment me when I don't check out a chick's ass.

Assuming that she is cool with the idea of sex with another woman, she will not allow anyone in the bedroom that she perceives to be better looking than her. If your wife has a self-confidence problem and sees herself as short, fat, buck-toothed, freckled, or otherwise deformed, she will only allow the most hideous of gremlins to suck your dick. You've got to get her thinking that she is hotter than Megan Fox, Jenna Jameson and a young, pre-disaster Brittany Spears combined. The way you do that depends on how ugly your wife is, but generally you do it by lying.

Many wives will ask us, "Do you think she's pretty?" Now, I don't deny that a woman is pretty if indeed I think she is, but I will always turn it around and show my wife how she compares favorably. I'll say that the chick's eyes are not as pretty as hers or something. I know it sounds stupid, but women still believe that we can distinguish their eyes from someone else's. There are some women I've met where it might have taken me a good fifteen minutes to notice that she even had eyes. It's just not relevant. You take two women and you flip them over and they pretty much look the same. Who gives a shit about their eyes?

A friend of mine convinced his wife that a threesome was a good idea, that it would be fun and everything, and they made plans to approach an acquaintance of hers. The mistake he made was not getting a picture of this chick that his wife had picked out. The description that she gave him was:

She's a tall blonde. She's in really good shape. I see her at the gym a lot. She is in her early twenties and she is single."

---

[5] When I see nice tits I take a look. How long depends on how nice.

What showed up at his door was a six-foot-four basketball forward with teeth like an old gorilla and the leg hair to match. What could he do but go through with it? To back out at the last minute would damage his chance with a real chick. Unfortunately, he blacked out during the festivities and his wife will not endure such embarrassment with another woman again. Sadly, my friend cries whenever they show WNBA highlights on TV and he complains of hair on his tongue that he just can't seem to spit out. Never commit to having sex with someone you have not seen. It seems like a no-brainer, but sometimes the promise of the threesome can cloud your sense of prudence.

If your woman is not the adventurous type, you might try to ease her into trying some new activities. One day I woke up to find a Groupon for a Korean vagina steam in my email box. I figured even if the wife didn't want to go, we could re-gift it to my sister-in-law, so I clicked.

My wife had never steamed her vagina before. It's not exactly mainstream in America yet (hence the Groupon). The shop uses these little wooden stools with holes in the middle. The ladies sit on the stools while a pot of tea is steaming underneath them for about twenty minutes. It is supposed to be very refreshing.

> I woke up to find a Groupon for a Korean vagina steam in my email box.

So I went to the shop with her so I could kinda check the whole scene out, but once she got called into the back I went next door to the sports bar for some wings. I'm sitting there thinking about what I'm going to do to her when I get her home, because I haven't had a really fresh vagina in a long time. A shower and a shave is one thing, but this was a full-on, deep steam cleansing. It's the difference between getting your car vacuumed and getting it <u>detailed</u>.

When I got her home, I was all over her before we even got out of the car. I actually had this romantic thought of doing it in the car, albeit while parked safely in our garage. I got her naked from the waist down and was delighted at the aroma. Her pussy smelled like my guitar case the first day I brought my Les Paul home. Erotic!

Then, my hopes were dashed as she exclaimed that she did not want to fool around so soon after the V steam. She did not want to lose the clean feeling.

Generally, I will do anything twice if it got me laid the first time. I won't *refuse* to do something just because it didn't get me laid the first time, but I definitely *will not* do anything again if was the exact cause of my blue balls. That's a rule. It's actually tattooed on my calf in Chinese.

But this V steam situation is different. I believe it was a springboard to some more daring behavior. There is not a direct line to a threesome, but my woman subsequently accompanied me to a Swedish death metal concert and was certified in scuba before the summer was over.

After years of reassuring her that she is beautiful, I realized that one of things that added to my wife's state of mind was the fact that I did not appear jealous of other men or self conscious of my own appearance. Somehow it makes her feel better to know that I am just as self-conscious as she is. So one night I asked her about a penile enlargement. We were at the movies, sitting there eating popcorn and Kit Kats, and I just blurted out, "I got an email for a penis enlargement. What do you think?" She looks around the theater, rearranges her coat in her lap, turns and looks at me with the biggest eyes I've ever seen and says to me, "No shit. I have been forwarding those emails to you for three years."

She went on you explain that she overheard something at a family Christmas party about my dad and my brother and she was confused about the apparent genetic favoritism. I hate that I know certain details about my family, but I assured my wife that she was not getting the short end of the stick[6].

At the risk of sounding like a complete ass, I must also note that neither my father nor my brother is the least bit masculine. My father speaks very softly, kind of like that dweeby arsonist in

---

[6] Pun very much intended.

Office Space[7]. I recall him trying to teach me to drive and he would mumble the whole time. "Yellow light... it's a soft shoulder over here... don't make eye contact with the bad motor scooter person." Then he'd make me attach the Club[8] to the steering wheel before going in to the mall.

My wife was apparently just kidding me anyway. But I let on like I was upset so that she could reassure me for a change. Frankly, I would never think of getting a penis enlargement. I am not completely sure how it works, but I do know that anything they could possibly do would only be cosmetic, and there is no way I would let anyone take a scalpel to my fully functional, and remarkably beautiful penis. The way I see it, my wife either thought it was so cute that I would be concerned about something like that, or she was flattered that I might undergo surgery for her. I win either way.

One of the biggest things that you need to convince your woman is that there is a difference between making love and fucking. Making love is an intimate sexual act that two people share in private. Fucking is a fun activity that any number of people can play at one time in any combination of males and females. It's exercise, like aerobics or kickboxing. In fact, it may even prolong your life by decreasing your risk of a heart attack. I am currently petitioning my Congressman, several members of the World Health Organization, and *Men's Fitness Magazine* to declare fucking a legitimate factor in reducing your chances of developing heart disease. Apparently, they need independent research to confirm my claims. If anyone would like to participate in a clinical study of the effects of massive amounts of sex on their ticker, please contact my publisher. They will put you in touch with me and we'll get the study underway ASAP.

Some fun things that you do with your wife should also be fun things that you can do with other people. For example, I like to play tennis. I like to play tennis with my wife. It just so happens that I also like to play tennis with other people as well.

---

[7] 20th Century Fox, 1999. If you haven't seen it before, just turn on TBS and wait a couple hours.

[8] This was a long, red bar that you locked to the steering wheel in the late 80's. Check out YouTube to see some of the old commercials. Very funny.

The biggest reason I play with others is that my wife sucks at tennis, and I want to play with someone who knows what they're doing. Of course, I don't tell her that. What I tell her is that I like the challenge of playing someone else that has different techniques, strategies, etc.

Similarly, I enjoy my wife's cooking. I know that she doesn't have to cook for me. She hasn't always cooked for me. It's something that I appreciate very much, and I tell her so every time I remember to. However, like many people, I like variety. I can only eat chicken so many different ways before I think, "Hey, is it going to kill me to have a little red meat every once in a while?" But my wife can't cook a steak, and her pork is a disaster, so if I want it, I have to get it on the outside. She doesn't seem to mind that I don't get the chicken when we go to a restaurant. Why should she mind that I want to invite some red meat into our bedroom?

Fucking and lovemaking are radically different, yet to the untrained eye they appear the same. Some may argue that physically they are the same, but emotionally and mentally they are different. I believe they are different on all three levels. When most people have sex with people they care about there are things going through their heads that enhance and detract from the experience. When you are just there to get off, you release yourself to the primal instincts within. The result is a potentially more physically satisfying lay.

You probably have had experiences like this with your partner. It happens a lot when you are pissed off at her but you get a chance to screw anyway, and you don't care to take all of that emotional bullshit into consideration.

Fucking is a physiological need that men have. It's the same urge that dogs get. We can't help it. We can't help that we think about sex every three minutes or whatever it is, and I for one can't control the fact that I need to get off a few times a week. Women shouldn't want to be simply an object to fulfill animal urges.

In ancient times, the highest class of women was above the duty of fulfilling their man's sexual needs. They had sex for procreation, for fun, and for love's sake, but to have to be on call every time a man's dick twitched would have been a big pain. I believe that my woman is of the highest possible class, so why should she subject herself to that? She shouldn't. Why should men try to suppress our highly evolved physiology? We shouldn't. The simple answer is the freedom to fuck. If John Adams and James Madison had any real foresight, it would have been in the Constitution.

Until your woman understands these critical differences between fucking and making love, her confidence will not be able to withstand the sight of you mounting another chick. The question really is, how do you go about communicating that message to her? That is where the importance of language skills comes in.

3: Language is Key

In the beginning stages of your mission it will always be inappropriate to say things like, "Her tits are looking tasty," or "I think what your friend needs is for me to give her a good tongue lashing." I cannot stress the importance of language enough. It seems like common sense, but men always seem to say stupid things at the wrong times. I believe that every man has had the opportunity to sleep with two women at once at some point in his life. Most of us are just too stupid to recognize the opportunity or we fail to make a move.

I further believe that the single biggest reason guys fail to make a move is that they can't think of what to say. In having spoken with many guys over the years about the subject, I have noticed that there are some situations that seem to happen to a lot of people. I have put together some scripts that will help you out should any of these particular situations present themselves in your own life. I encourage you to read them out loud, as written, several times. In doing so, try and internalize the ideas behind the words rather than the script itself. I think we have all been in a situation where we have over-prepared what we were going to say to someone and it comes off sounding rehearsed. Remember, you don't want your wife to think that you are one of those freaks who reads books like this and has been planning his dialogue over the course of five years.

Situation # 1: The Sleepover

This scenario is where your wife's friend comes to visit from out of town. The best is when it is a friend from college, 'cause college girls do wild things[9] and maybe, if you're lucky, one of them did some wild things, or, even better, maybe the two of them did wild things together. You will no doubt entertain your

---

[9] I highly recommend the movie *Wild Things* with Denise Richards, Neve Campbell, and Matt Dillon. It has nothing to do with your wife's college friends, but it is highly sexual with multiple scenes of hot women making out.

guest in the evening with dinner, perhaps drinks, and some pleasant conversation. Assuming this woman is a suitable sex partner, try to work the following dialogue into the conversation.

"So I bet you girls did some wild stuff back in the day, huh? Why don't you tell me about the craziest thing you two did together."

Now, if they tell you about something good like an orgy at the frat house or screwing under the bleachers, you struck gold. Keep the ball rolling with this little gem:

"Wow, you girls weren't kidding when you said you were crazy. It's too bad you can't recapture a little bit of that youth. Stuff like that just doesn't happen as often as it should anymore."

If, instead, they tell you a story about an all night study session when they accidentally set the drapes on fire, then you need to say something like this:

"If that is the craziest story you have to tell, then you girls haven't lived a full life yet. I know you wish you were sitting there telling me about sex in public places or stealing the rival's mascot or something. If you want crazy, I'll show you crazy."

At this point you have to show them something. You have a multitude of options.

1. You could kiss your woman passionately with the hope of having sex in front of what's-her-face.
2. You could kiss what's-her-face.
3. You could get naked.

Any of these will get a reaction out of them. Personally, I like the first one. It's not dangerous, and it has possibilities if you keep pushing for the kiss to lead somewhere. The other two options are definitely ballsy and show your commitment to this project. Given the context of the conversation preceding your move, you shouldn't get in too much long-term trouble; however, you might piss off your woman and make her friend's visit a bit uncomfortable.

A great way to approach your overnight guest in a less direct way is to allow her to witness you and your wife having sex. Put on a show for her and she might leap from the audience onto the stage. Failing that, you will at least spark her interest and bringing up the topic in conversation will be easier the following day.

> If you're too self-conscious to have sex with your wife while someone else is watching, then how do you expect to do it with someone else participating?

I've read about this in *Penthouse* a million times. The way to do it is simply to leave your bedroom door ajar. Your woman may check to see that the door is closed before she proceeds with intercourse with another person in the house, so you have to be sneaky and reopen it after she has closed it. Drop your condom on her side of the bed and ask her to look for it. Meanwhile you are out of bed and cracking the door. If you don't use condoms, pretend to hear a noise in the hall and go check it out. When she asks if you shut the door you think to yourself, "Of course I didn't, now turn around and bury your face in that pillow so you won't see your friend spying on us while I give it to you." But instead you say, "Uh, yeah."

Remember that in order to get her friend's attention you may need to make more noise that you usually do during sex. Pounding the wall with your fist is good. Lots of "Oh, Baby's" are good. Don't be shy. If you're too self-conscious to have sex with your wife while someone else is watching, then how do you expect to do it with someone else participating?

Many times your guest will be sleeping on the sofa in the living room. No one ever sleeps well on a sofa at someone else's house. Besides the smelly, lumpy heap that you are made to lay on, there are weird noises coming from the clocks, the appliances, the neighbors, and the settling house. If you were to get up for something in the refrigerator wearing only your underwear, making a racket with the pickle jar and slamming drawers, she will notice you.

Another thing that will help you get noticed is a raging hard-on poking out of your boxers. I swear to you if anything in this book is true, it is this—if you have any shot of getting that woman in bed with you, she will be intrigued by your exhibition. If it doesn't spark some interest, then it was never going to happen. If you sense some curiosity on her part, talk to her. Walk yourself over to her and start a conversation. Watch her try and not look. Even better, watch her stare. Then you'll know you have one less female to convince.

Situation #2: The Waitress

I find that as I get older, I meet fewer and fewer new women. I know that they are out there. The hospitals are full of new babies being born and the high schools are graduating new chicks every year. There is a seemingly endless supply, and yet, I seem to be meeting fewer of them. It's a drag.

Fortunately, there are hot women working in everyday jobs, running everyday errands and you will encounter them. Seize those opportunities!

Imagine you are out for dinner with your wife at a nice restaurant and the hostess is a hottie. Forget about her. You don't have enough time to pull off that maneuver, Maverick. She is going to ask you how many people are in your party and what your name is. You don't have a slick enough answer to either of those questions that has any hope of engaging her. At least not while your wife is riding in Goose's seat.

So you can check out her ass while she leads you and the wife to your table, and then graciously accept the menu she hands you. Before you know it, the waitress comes over to introduce herself and she ends up being hot, too!

Waitresses are great prospects. They are nicer to you if they think they can make money off you, but they are not as cold and calculating about it as your typical stripper. I have found that if I spend a little money, and show them that I am there to have a good time, it's easy to draw them in.

1. Start out by asking what appetizers she recommends. Appetizers are not expensive but your inquiry will send the message that you are there to spend money.
2. Don't order a beer unless you are at a brew pub. Beer at a nice restaurant is low class. I resist the recent trend suggesting the contrary, as if being brewmaster was something that required a college education. Beer connoisseurs make me laugh. I mean, I can blather on and on about how different orange juices taste different, come from various oranges and regions of the world. It's still just orange juice. And I'm sorry, but I can't get the image of frat boys drinking from a funnel out of my mind. Beer is not going to impress anyone.
3. Don't order wine unless you want to get an expensive bottle. Ordering a $6 glass of Shiraz actually makes you look cheap when there are $10 options and wines sold by the bottle.
4. Instead of beer or wine, order a cocktail and specify your top shelf liquor. I like to order a Grey Goose martini dirty, and I look at the waitress like I am Ricky Martin when I say the word, "dirty."
5. When it comes time to order your entrée, tell the waitress you are considering two options and ask for her opinion. I don't always take her recommendation, but I use it as a conversation starter. I may ask her which menu selection is <u>really bad</u>. This is usually a fun question because she will always have some dish in mind she doesn't like but she may be reluctant to reveal it to you. Playfully pull it out of her.

"So if the filet is great and the swordfish is great, what on the menu is really bad? What's the worst thing on here? I promise I won't tell anyone else."

Throughout the course of the evening, I like to engage the waitress with some conversation starters, but I also want to keep my woman involved. To achieve this, I start a conversation with my wife that easily transitions into a comment or question for the waitress.

To the wife: *"I saw on The Today Show that animal prints are in fashion this season."*

Let the conversation flow with your wife. Even if it doesn't sustain itself until the waitress shows up, you can always reverse course and bring the subject up again when the waitress returns to check on your drinks.

To the waitress: *"Has management ever considered adding a leopard print scarf to your server uniform? (pause for her answer) I think it could be very flattering to your skin tone. Amy Robach[10] was raving about the new fall fashions last week and I heard leopard prints are hot right now."*

Here are a few more starters. Obviously, develop some of your own that can also get your wife and the waitress talking and having a fun time.

#1
"Who do you like in the next Ultimate Fighting Championship?"
　　"Who's fighting?"
"It's me against one of the busboys at McCormick & Schmick's."
　　"I'm not much into bloodsports."
"Well, you could have fooled me. I have a very keen eye for wrestlers. I bet you could clean up in a cage fight."

#2
"How come they don't have more airlines with live TV to watch on the plane?"
　　"Is that important to you?"
"I think you'd get a lot more guys flying during the NCAA tournament if they knew they wouldn't miss the games, and I'll never fly on New Year's Day just because I know I'll miss like five bowl games."

---

[10] Natalie Morales or Amy Robach? It's like the Beatles or Elvis, Coke or Pepsi. I'm partial to Amy. I would watch her do a report about paint drying and love every minute of it.

#3

"I'm thinking about changing careers and wonder if I could get your input."

"Okay, what do you want to do?

"I want to be a forensic geometrist."

"That's not a real occupation."

"Yes, it is. I will use geometry to solve crimes. Sometimes the police need to know the trajectory of bullets and they use a forensic geometrist to apply the Pythagorean Theorem and find the killer."

Remember that your wife is with you at the table, so you can't use the same material with every waitress at every restaurant you visit. She is going to hear this and wonder what the heck you are doing? Be sure to mix it up.

There are two schools of thought on closing the deal in the waitress scenario. I think you have to close the deal with the waitress on the first night. Other intelligent people believe that you should begin frequenting the restaurant in an attempt to build a closer relationship with her. Let's examine each option.

If you attempt to close her on the first night and you fail, you have only lost the time and money that you were going to spend at the restaurant anyway. You will walk away having no homework, no worries and nothing to cloud your mind going forward. With that in mind, you can go for broke. When the check comes, ask her if she wants to come back to your place for drinks when she gets off work.

Of course, it's possible that you end up leaving a good prospect that would have gone home with you after just one or two more encounters. I have had women tell me that they absolutely will not go home with someone that they have just met that night.

If you try to build a relationship as a regular, you have to spend more money and take time to go back. I can foresee such a plan getting very expensive. Additionally, the opportunity cost is the possibility that another, more agreeable woman is waiting tables at another restaurant. Rather than become a regular at the restaurant, just hope that you bump into her somewhere. In that way, you're meeting could be categorized as serendipitous and lead to something exciting, as opposed to calculated and potentially awkward.

Situation#3: The Showoff

There are no doubt situations where your woman will bring you to her place of business and introduce you to her co-workers. She may disguise the reason by saying that she needs you to pick her up because her car broke down, or she needs to have emergency dental work performed, but the real reason for you coming will be for her to show you off to the people at her office.

Women may deny it, but I believe they talk about sex when we aren't around. I believe they brag about our charm and prowess just as often as they complain about our apathy and ignorance. When the time comes and you are summoned to her place of business, try out a script such as the following.

"Hello, ladies. (Enter wife's name here) has told me a lot about you; however, she failed to mention how beautiful her co-workers were. I see now why it's taken here this long to bring me by. She obviously didn't trust me in the presence of so many attractive women. (Pause for giggling or gagging as the case may be).

There is something about addressing chicks as ladies that I have found to be remarkably effective in charming them. This situation is a perfect example of when to employ such a tactic. The dictionary defines a lady as a woman of high social position; refined and classy. A chick is noted as slang and "often offensive" and merely defined as a young woman. Most guys don't care enough to differentiate between the two in their own speech, but chicks seem to notice. Think of it this way—ten guys come up to them that day and you are the only one to address them as ladies. That is going to stand out in their minds. You are now memorable.

Sidenote: the word chickenshit is actually in the dictionary defined as –n. 1. Petty or trivial details, tasks, or the like. –adj. 2.

obsessed with petty details. 3. menial or petty. 4. cowardly.[11] Remember when you would be doing your homework as a kid, and instead of looking up words you needed for your essay, you tried to find swear words in the dictionary? The best I ever came across when I was a kid was "bitch," but now there are tons of them in there.

I wouldn't recommend actually following through with a sexual encounter with a co-worker of your wife's. The reasons for avoiding that situation are described later in the book, but what you can achieve here is a possible participant in a sexual encounter later on in your plan. People do leave their jobs for better opportunities. Keep track of that interested individual and if she or your woman leaves the company, then she becomes a hot prospect.

Situation 4: The Soccer Mom

It's a sad fact, but 50% of all marriages end in divorce. The next time you are at your kid's soccer game or ballet recital, look around for the hot moms. Statistically speaking, half of them are either single or will be available eventually.

My son played soccer for a couple years when he was five and six years old. I paced the sidelines and made a lot of good contacts with the moms. The key with this crowd is not to move too fast. It's not like picking up the waitress in one night. You will see these women many times, and in some cases, you will see them over the course of many years as your kids reunite on future teams.

Your play is basically to become friends with them, not flirt. Never flirt on the soccer field. You are surrounded by prospects and some of them will be turned off if they see you flirting with others. Some will forever carry that memory of you in their mind and you will never have a shot with them again. All you want to do is get to know these women at the games.

---

[11] Random House Webster's College Dictionary, 2007

31

> Give her the impression that you are an involved father. Moms eat that shit up.

Every mother wants to talk about her kid and wants to hear other parents praise her kid. So the introduction is pretty simple.

"Hi. Which kid is yours?"

She may point out one of the kids that excels at that particular activity. Hope that she doesn't. If the kid is good, your interest in the child won't be unique enough for her to fully appreciate it. If she points out a kid that is average in ability, come back with this:

"Oh, sure, I have seen him play. He (really hustles/always seems like he is having fun/scored a goal/whatever)!"

She will most likely start opening up about how her son does this or that and drone on for a while. If she is polite, she'll ask you which child is yours and give you an opportunity to talk for a bit. Now you have engaged her. Introduce yourself. She will reciprocate. You are no longer strangers.

I like to give the conversation a rest at this point. I feign interest in the game but I'm actually imagining the soccer mom naked. The purpose of the silence is to throw her off my scent so that when I restart the conversation it won't seem like I am forcing it. When I break the silence after about five minutes, I might ask her one of the following questions:

"Which school does_____ go to?"

"Do you have other kids that play _____?"

Either of these will lead to more questions and probably return questions from her. Keep talking and developing familiarity with this woman. Give her the impression that you are an involved father. Moms eat that shit up.

If the soccer mom is married or has a serious boyfriend, you need to keep her in a holding pattern. Visit with her when you see her at the games or around town, but don't move too hard on her. Ideally, you'll have several married women circling your tower. Then, as they get divorced (or separated), then you can light up the runway and bring them in.

Let's now assume you discover the soccer mom is single. Invite her over to your place for a Saturday night play date. She brings her kid over and you and your wife make dinner and watch a movie. When the kids are playing and the three adults are alone, start out by complimenting her kid.

"Your (son/daughter) is so (friendly/smart/cute)! I just can't believe it!"

You're priming the pump with these compliments for the kid. She is accepting the compliment and internalizing it as her own. Once you have established that her kid is great, start complimenting her directly.

"When I first met you, I thought you were too young to have a child that old."

As trite as this compliment may seem, I have never seen it fail. Women never get tired of hearing it. When she responds with the inevitable purring, lay your thing down.

"Do you ever get to cut loose when (kid's name)'s father has him for the weekend? You should come out with (wife/girlfriend) and me."

There are certain words that are universally held in high esteem. When spoken, these words convey positive messages. We must use them to our advantage. We must exploit them for our own personal gain. The word "sharing" is a good word. We have been conditioned since childhood that it is good to share. Consequently, we always try and share as much as we can, lest we be seen as selfish. So, when speaking to your wife about a threesome, don't tell her that you want to have a threesome. You must tell her that you think it would be nice to share her with another woman. The same is true about the word pleasure. Pleasures are simple, they are innocent. What kind of heartless bitch would deprive someone of pleasure?

Just as important as knowing what to say is knowing when to keep your fool mouth shut. What we need is for you to get conditioned to stay silent after hearing certain phrases. You've heard them before, and undoubtedly you've fucked up the answers before. Some common fatal questions are:

"What do you think of my father?"

"How fat would I have to get before you would leave me?"

"You like her boobs better than mine, don't you?"

"If she were here right now, which one of us would you want to have sex with first?"

Don't answer any of that shit. What I like to do is fake an accident. When she asks me anything like that, I'll drop a turkey leg on my shirt, dump my drink on the table—whatever. It makes a big mess which you must excuse your self to go clean up. Remember this line:

"Honey, I want to get this stain out before it sets."

If my wife thinks it's odd for me to be so concerned about the appearance of my tattered, 1987 AFC Championship T-shirt, she has never questioned it to my face. I have also faked my contact lens popping out, accidentally getting horseradish sauce in my eye, and abdominal pain in order to escape answering such questions. I used to keep a can of fart spray in the toilet tank and whenever the situation warranted I would explain that I had to take a massive dump. I would then go into the bathroom (with the sports section) and wait it out. The stench was so overpowering that she wouldn't come near me for at least an hour after I was out.

Another approach I like to use is one that I learned from that Robert Redford movie, *All the President's Men*. Remember when Woodward and Berstein were trying to get the players in the Watergate scandal to respond to their stories in the Washington Post? The men questioned would give what they called a "non-denial denial." It went something like this:

Woodward: *"Mr. Corrupt Government Official, was Haldeman overseeing the payoffs?"*

Mr. Corrupt Government Official: *"These charges have been deemed outrageous by high ranking officials, and furthermore, you have no business even printing such things."*

So when your woman asks if she is fat, you use a non-denial denial:

Your Woman: *"Do you think I'm fat?"*

You: *"Honey, none of your friends would say that you are fat. If you were fat, then why would you get all those looks on the street? How can you even say something like that?*

See, you didn't say one way or another what you thought about it. If she's not satisfied with your answers, you just keep dancing around the issue until she's dizzy and gives up asking. If the dancing wears you out, bust out the fart spray.

Another important thing to remember is that you need to make sure that no matter what she says, no matter how stupid it is, you pretend that it's the most intelligent damn thing you have ever heard in your whole life. Say, for example, that you are watching the Super Bowl, and your wife says to you,

"They shouldn't call those long passes bombs. It's too negative and it adds an even more violent image to an already overly violent sport. What they should name them is something like 'the dream toss.'"

Really try and avoid making a face, choke back the bile filling your mouth, and calmly reply with something like the following:

"Yes, Sweetums, they actually called it that for a while back in the seventies, but it lost favor when the Native Americans started making a ruckus about using their culture as a means for hyping our already overblown sporting events. As it turns out, 'dream toss' is a Chippewa term for nocturnal emission. It's quite sacred and they didn't like the Pittsburgh Steelers cheapening the whole thing. So out of respect for those whose lands on which we play, we reluctantly refer to those long passes as bombs. That was a marvelous point you made though, about the violence and how we don't need to be violent, because... you know, we hate violence for some reason. That was great."

Another example that might come up more often is when she is describing a problem with the car. Perhaps this is a familiar situation for you. She says something half-witted, but rather than point out her obvious flaws, you shower her with sarcastic praise.

Her: *"Honey, there is something wrong with the car. It isn't accelerating as quickly as it used to and it makes kind of a grinding noise when it's moving."*

You: *"Yeah, oh. I'm surprised you were able to pick up on that, Dear. Actually, that sounds like I (meaning her) left the parking brake on. Good thing you noticed that. Thanks."*

Intimacy is something that women always want more of, and they can never seem to get enough of it. I, like many men, feel like intimacy is over-rated and too often preempts Monday Night Football, a good bean dip, and time on my recliner. My wife tells me that I feel that way because I am no good at it. Since my wife didn't write a book, her opinion doesn't count; however, I wanted to throw an idea out to those readers who do have problems being intimate with their women.

One way to manufacture some intimacy is to whisper. I swear whispering is very effective if you want to come across sounding intimate. You can whisper anything and it will sound good. It creates a feeling of closeness. Whisper the following sentences and see if it doesn't put you in an erotic mood.

"Don't hog the potatoes."

"I didn't shower yet this morning, because I didn't want to miss Sportscenter."

"That damn mailman always delivers late on Saturdays."

Now you can't go around whispering this kind of stuff. It was for illustrative purposes only, but hopefully you got the idea. When something worthy of a whisper comes up in conversation—whisper it.

4: It's Give and Take

What I am about to suggest to you is not within the capacity of many of you reading this. It goes against the animal instincts inside us that have evolved over thousands of years. It will challenge your very commitment to this project. Do not doubt that just because you cannot go through with what I will propose that you are men. I admit that it stinks of absolute lunacy. To condemn my proposal as a pinko, commie scheme to undermine America and sabotage our values is perfectly rational. But like they say, desperate times call for desperate measures. I guess it's just a question of how desperate you are.

I don't want to dance around it any more, so I will just come right out with it. If you allow your woman to sleep with another man, you may increase your chances of getting her together with another woman.

Some women just don't have a natural lust for other women. I dare to say that most women, in fact, do not, and consequently, those women are harder to convince that sex with chicks is a good idea. Women do, however, have a natural lust for men. It is this natural lust for men that you must cultivate. Yes, I said cultivate. You must create an environment where she feels comfortable expressing her attraction to other men in hopes that she will desire to sleep with other men. From there we can change her point of view from lusting after attractive men to lusting after attractive people. After all, women are the fairer sex and in time we hope that she will see the beauty in women.

In order for your wife to sleep with another woman she has two hurdles to overcome. First, she has never slept with a female before. There's nothing we can do about that one. Second, she has never slept with anyone outside of your happily monogamous relationship. In order to accept sleeping with another man, she will only have to clear the one hurdle of sleeping with someone outside of your relationship. In doing so, this same hurdle is cleared for our primary objective as well. Obviously, this reasoning only works if your wife has remained faithful. If not, skip ahead.

I believe it is possible to make the transition from finding other men attractive to lusting after women without her having to actually have intercourse with another man, but there isn't a logical progression from one to the other. Having said that, I think you have to expect that some physical activity is necessary. Generally, I would say anything involving one or more parties completely exposing their genital areas will result in a satisfactory clearing of the hurdle.

Now, I understand that a lot of you are wondering what the hell kind of fucked up scheme this is, so I want to lay out the plan very clearly. There is a clear progression of events that we are looking for. First, your woman should begin communicating her attraction to other men to you in confidence. This is an intimate communication that must be met by seemingly unwavering support from you. Second, she begins to reveal her attraction to other men openly. This is merely innocent flirtation, but the freedom that she feels will fuel her sexual excitement. Next, the two of you begin talking about her acting on her sexual desires. If she doesn't initiate, then perhaps you should ask her if she is interested in fooling around with one of the objects of her attention. At this point you will have to work out with her whether or not you will be present, how the activity will be initiated, and all the other crucial details. Then, and brace yourself, she goes out and fools around with another guy.

Following her activities, you should suggest to her that you would like to experiment sexually with her and another woman. At her probable objection you explain to that her recent encounter was with someone outside of your marriage, and you would like the two of you to try something similar. You might tell her that you would feel more comfortable if she was there with you.

For this to work it is imperative that you maintain control while still providing her with the illusion of total freedom. You want to control who she messes around with, where and when it happens, and whether or not you are present. This is tricky. If she is interested in someone that she knows from a restaurant she eats lunch at during the week, you might not have an opportunity to exert some influence on him. At the same time, if that is who she chooses, then you might have to allow her to pursue it in order to achieve your long-term goal. But I think the best strategy is to help her think of people you are at least somewhat familiar with.

There is another way to approach this, and it might be one that popped into your head when you first began to read this section. Your wife has now experienced the ultimate sexual freedom and you were the one who granted it to her. If she doesn't expect some reciprocity, then she is naïve as all hell. In the event that she does not

> If she doesn't expect some reciprocity, then she is naïve as all hell.

shortly after her experience offer a similar opportunity for you, it will be necessary to implement Plan B.

Plan B, simply stated, is where you lobby for equal treatment under the law. Again, language is the key to your success. Obviously, I mention this as a backup plan if you were to use it at all, because it is a tad manipulative. It may seem logical to you and I, but female logic is much different and you might end up pissing her off.

A very close friend of mine implemented this very strategy not long ago. It did not go exactly as he had planned, and looking back we both agree it was because he moved immediately to Plan B. As I recount his story, imagine your plan in your head and how things can quickly take a turn for the worst. As always, names have been changed because our women would kill us if they knew we were writing about this sort of thing.

Tony is married to a very attractive woman. Her name is Teri. Teri watched her figure and liked to work out at the gym. She went through the whole routine, and I'm telling you Teri is smoking hot. After their first baby, Teri had a tough time losing the last of her pregnancy pounds and she sought out the expertise of a personal trainer at her gym. After Teri's first day with her new trainer, Tony could tell that she was very impressed with the gentleman. His name was Jim. She was going on and on about his credentials as a trainer, his great body, the excellent workout he devised for her, and so on.

Over the next couple weeks, as Teri worked out, Tony would hear Jim's name over and over in conversation. It was pretty obvious that she had a little crush on this guy. When she was telling him about her workouts she would just be bouncing up and down as she spoke. So one night Tony asked Teri if she thought Jim was an attractive man. She thought for a moment, but said, "yes." Then, Tony asked her if she thought he was sexy. She said without hesitation, "oh, yeah." The conversation went on from there and Tony eventually gave her the go ahead to sleep with the guy.

In his mind he was thinking that he hit the jackpot, because upon her return it would be his turn to sleep with someone else. Teri, however, did not see it that way. Tony requested some tit for tat and some goose for the gander, and she accused him of only allowing her to explore her sexual desire with Jim so he could have someone of his own. Now, of course, she's right, but that's not an epiphany we want any of our wives or girlfriends having. Before, you were just an immature idiot with a fantasy, but now you're a manipulative asshole.

5: Finding the Right Woman

Finding the right woman can seem like a real-life "Where's Waldo" game. You look out into the crowded world and you've got to pick out some chick who will not only sleep with you, but also possesses some intangible quality that will meet with the approval of your wife. Unfortunately, she probably isn't wearing a red stocking cap and big round glasses.

Before you begin your search for the right woman you may want to be aware of the different varieties of bi-sexuals. In the simplest possible breakdown there are two stereotypes that emerge: butch and femme. The butch lesbian is the one that plays the more masculine role, and the femme plays a more feminine role. From these two very general descriptions one will find many subcategories of lesbians, including butchy femme, sport dyke, soft butch, bulldagger, barracuda femme, lipstick dagger, etc. The list is never ending and the differentiation between subcategories becomes increasingly harder to quantify. In order to master the terminology that is ever evolving in the homosexual culture, I would have to immerse myself in that culture for a period of months, possibly years. That is the kind of undercover work to which I am just not committed, and frankly it really isn't necessary.

My favorite architect, Louis Sullivan,[12] once said, "form follows function." He was referring to buildings, but his astute observation is easily translated to the subject of lesbians. Louie knew that if he saw a lesbian with a flat-top wearing construction boots, she was butch. He also knew that if he saw one in a short red dress, high heels and too much make-up, she was a lipstick femme. These physical characteristics are a reflection of their function. The butch lesbian appears more masculine, more aggressive and if you were to sleep with her you should expect her to behave in such a manner. Likewise, a lipstick femme appears slutty and her behavior would most likely coincide.

---

[12] More specifically, Sullivan is the only architect that I know of that said anything that I could somehow relate to lesbians.

These are not hard and fast rules and many lesbians do not fit neatly into these stereotypical models, so again I hesitate to say that you should seek out a chick based on these classifications.

A better strategy would be to hunt for a chick based on the degree to which you are familiar with them. There are two schools of thought here. You an either try and find someone that you know who may be receptive to the idea, or you can find a stranger. Let's examine each one separately.

First of all, someone you know is great because you can gauge her potential acceptance to the idea. You would probably not approach a woman you know that is married with three children. That is not to say that married women never do this sort of thing, but for your purposes they are not the best prospects. They have to deal with their husbands, or worse yet, if the husband finds out what you did with his wife, you may have to deal with the husbands. It can get messy, so my advice is to find single chicks.

Someone you know may also have a great personality that leads you to believe that she may be willing to do something with you and your woman. Perhaps she speaks about her many lovers in casual conversation. Perhaps she dresses like she's ready for sex at any moment. Maybe you just want to pick out someone that you have always thought would be dynamite lay. I would caution you, though, that if your woman is aware of your fascination with this chick that it could hurt your chances of success. Women do not want to be one-upped in bed with their husbands. If you come across as just wanting to screw this other woman, it ain't never gonna happen.

Conversely, someone you know can be bad because if they turn you down there may be some awkward moments to follow. Never approach someone that you know before you have at least tentatively approved the idea with your wife. If that person is not into it, they may be inclined to say something to your woman and then you're screwed.

Having sex with someone you know is also dangerous because of the possibility that something embarrassing happens in the bedroom. Imagine having to see that person again on a regular basis. For example, say you ask one of her friends and she agrees. You are in the bedroom doing whatever and say that something embarrassing happens. I don't care what, but something embarrassing has happened to all of us at some point or another (if you don't recall anything embarrassing it is because of a complex defense mechanism in the upper cortex of your brain that has evolved over time[13]).

Say, for example, you are giving oral sex to her friend while your woman sucks you off and at the point of your orgasm you inadvertently bite down on some flesh and break the skin. It hurts like a bitch and she screams for you to turn on the light. You all tumble off one another and stagger to the lightswitch. Upon inspection of her wound she discovers that she is bleeding profusely. She tries unsuccessfully for a few moments to try and stop the bleeding at which point you all agree she needs to see a doctor. She's in no condition to drive, so naturally you volunteer to drive her and your wife comes along. As awkward as it would be at the emergency room answering the nurse's questions, it would be doubly awkward seeing this woman in church, at the next tee-ball game or in line at the post office.

> I've gone into Mario Tricoci just to scout out bored housewives that might have nothing to do after their make-over.

Do not even think about asking someone that you work with. You will be flirting with disaster. If she's not into it, you're looking at sexual harassment lawsuits, gossip, and expulsion from the ranks of the promotable by your Judeo-Christian man bosses. Don't let your wife ask one of her co-workers either. Suppose she is successful. The situation is now out of your control. The men at her office are likely to find out and then they see it as an opportunity to move on her. I mentioned before that your wife with another man might be a means to an end, but these men are not under your thumb. Another consequence if she is not successful is that she may quit

---

[13] The preceding conclusion has no basis in science, fact or common sense.

her job in embarrassment and then you'll be supporting her ass instead of screwing it.

Strangers are good prospects. The reason, quite simply, is that if they say no and they think you are a freak, who cares? You'll never see them again. They're disposable. It really expands your pool of available women, too. Now everyone in line at the grocery store is a prospect. I've gone into Mario Tricoci just to scout out bored housewives that might have nothing to do after their make-over. I highly recommend the day spa market. Those women spend the bucks to keep themselves looking good, so 56% of them are do-able. If they are there during the middle of the day, it's likely they don't have jobs, and chicks without jobs are a different breed. My last study on the sex drive of unemployed women found that they are 72% more likely to have sex in the middle of the day that those women who held a job.[14]

Maybe you have found someone you'd like to proposition, but you're not quite sure yet. I always find that if there is scientific evidence to back up what my gut is telling me, I am more likely to take action. Here are two ideas to help confirm your intuition about a prospect.

First, consider the woman's birth order. This is the order in which they were born to their parents. It is generally agreed that first-borns make the best threesome prospects. They are likely to need the approval of others and respond well to compliments. If there is something that allows you to at least appear genuine in your flattery, then you have an angle. You want to give her a little line and let her run. She'll then talk more about herself and the accomplishments which had you so impressed. Now you start reeling her in with your body language. Lean in. Stare deep into her eyes and nod slightly.

This is where you watch for her to get close enough to the boat so you can hit her over the head with an oar. If she continues to go on and talk about herself AND if she appears to believe that you are impressed with her, keep going. Find something on her face that is attractive. Eyes, nose and chin

---

[14] The study was conducted at a mall in suburban Chicago. Shoppers were propositioned at random and their employment status was confirmed.

It is generally agreed that first-borns make the best threesome prospects. They are likely to need the approval of others and respond well to compliments.

seem to work the best. Don't use the lips because that can be taken as sexual too early in the conversation. Let's suppose you like this woman's nose (or at least it's plausible that someone might find her nose attractive). Tell her the following:

"Your nose is absolutely perfect. Has anyone ever told you that?"

Notice nothing is sexual yet. My comment may be odd, but it's not creepy.

"Me and my wife (girlfriend) were just talking about noses the other night. I don't know how we got on the topic, but we were talking about noses. You know, what makes a cute nose and what doesn't. You have a beautiful nose. You could be a nose model."

At this point she will appear flattered, confused, or repulsed. These are the only outcomes I have witnessed. If she is repulsed, abort mission. If it's either of the other two, continue.

She may ask what a nose model does. This is a buying signal. It's like she just took off her panties and plugged your address into her Garmin.

"Nose models pose for photos with Breathe Right Nasal Strips, nasal sprays or those sticky strips that you use to remove blackheads."

Still not overtly sexual yet. But now comes the oar to the skull.

"We should get together sometime—you me and (wife or girlfriend). I'm going to tell her I found the nose of the century. Have you been to that new wine bar on Central Street?"

Second-borns are a nightmare. They tend to be argumentative and want to critique everything. Third–borns are known for experimenting with new things and can be good prospects. My main concern with them is emotional. They can be clingy and their feelings get hurt when you usher them out of the apartment immediately afterwards. I'd rather not have the inconvenience.

Handwriting analysis is another way to weed through the women. Unfortunately, there is only so much you can glean without getting a full-page handwriting sample. Often, that is not possible unless she is in your fifth period history class, so I will only point out what to look for in the small samples. These can be found in Post-it notes, grocery lists, or Scattergories game sheets.

Unfortunately, there is no reliable way to determine a woman's homosexual tendencies merely from a handwriting sample. What we can ascertain is her level of sexuality.

Handwriting can be divided into three zones. The middle zone is where you see the a, e, o, u, s, w, and the letters that make up the center of the line. The upper zone contains the top of the letters b, k, l, h and those that have loops extending above the middle zone. The lower zone contains the bottoms of the letters p, g, j, q, and letters that have loops extending below the middle zone.

It is the lower zone that is of particular interest to the horny male. Take a good look at the loops in the lower zone. Long, full loops indicate a very sensual personality. Slim or short loops are created by bitter, frigid women.

Compare the two samples in figure 1. The top sample has a very full loop on the y. Whoever wrote that one must be horny as all hell. The bottom sample has a very small, thin loop on the g. Relative to the top part of the g in the middle zone, the loop is miniscule. The woman who wrote this sample is clearly not a sexual person. She collects Chia pets, watches all five hours of

The Office on TBS each night and is afraid to look men in the eye on the street.

Figure 1.

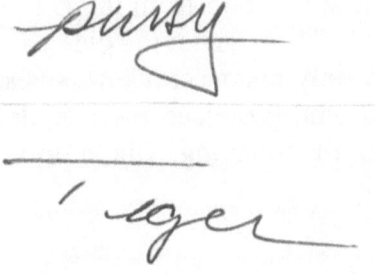

Evidence of heavy pressure on the writing instrument is a positive sign. You will see thick, dark lines in the writing and this is indicative of someone with a lot of energy. They will have a physical drive that can sometimes manifest itself in sexual aggressiveness.

I love the aggressive ones. It saves so much time. When a woman will turn and face me as I walk in the room, I can immediately narrow my focus. When she turns her head slightly and eyefucks me as I walk to the bar, I know to ask the bartender to give me an extra drink for the lady over there. As I wait for the drinks, I don't have to scan my brain for a good opening line. She's saved me a tremendous amount of mental energy. I'm just going to walk over there and say the following:

"I wanted to come over and tell you how much I appreciate sexual assertiveness in a woman. I may be a bit old-fashioned, but I would love to share a drink with you and get to know each other. Then we can head out and do all sorts of nasty things to each other."

That seems to work pretty well. Especially with the cougar crowd.

There's one more thing you can find in handwriting samples that can lead you to raise a prospect's standing in your search for the right woman. Every so often you can find sexual messages within the overall picture. When you view a writing sample, let your eyes look at the page as a painting rather than words to be read. Sometimes you can see distinct images. Occasionally, these images are overtly sexual.

Take a look at figure 2. See how the loop from the L raises up to rest on the loops in the G's? There are no accidents, no coincidences in one's handwriting; only unconscious missives to the observant reader. The woman who produced the sample in figure 2 is undoubtedly interested in titty-fucking. She'd do it all day and night if she could.

Figure 2.

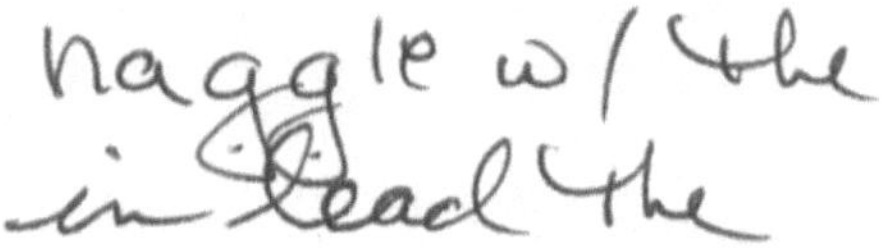

nagg1e w/ the
in tead the

Let's talk about diseases. When you are engaging in sex with complete strangers you run the very real risk of getting an incurable virus. I don't mean to minimize the risk with acquaintances, because despite what you may think, you do not know who has them. Just because you know someone well, and your impression of her is that she would always insist on using condoms does not mean she is disease free. Use a condom yourself for the simple reason that sex with multiple women is not worth risking your life.[15] If that is not reasoning enough, then do it for your wife. Women seem to think that sex without out a condom is more personal. If you use a condom with other women, but go bareback with her, it gives her something over these other women and may help the two of you maintain intimacy even when someone else is there. Similarly, she should use condoms when fucking other guys. Just another tidbit I thought I'd add: I heard on one of those radio sex shows that you can get HIV from kissing someone. It is not from saliva, but rather from bloody gums. It seems that when people brush their

---

[15] Such common sense advice makes this book more acceptable to politically correct book stores and the corporate deadheads that operate them.

teeth, as they often do before a date, they create tiny abrasions on their gums that secrete blood. If both parties have recently brushed their teeth there is the possibility of a virus transferal. I'm just telling you what I heard. A responsible author would check the accuracy of such things before printing them, but I will instead refer you to the legal disclaimer on page 8.

Another potential problem is pregnancy. Whatever your attitude is regarding abortion, you have no way of knowing what your new sexual partners' attitudes are. If you get a strange woman pregnant she may choose to have a baby to whom you have a financial responsibility. Think about the potential nightmare if your wife becomes pregnant and you aren't sure if it is yours or another man's child. Do you then abort a baby that may be your own? Even if you are certain that the child is not yours (if you had a vasectomy, for example), would your wife abort her child? These are all questions that you do not want to have to answer.

6: Seek the Wisdom of Others

There is really no point in trying to reinvent the wheel. If you find someone who has accomplished the ultimate, you should pick his brain for every scrap of useful knowledge. Ask him how he got started, what opportunities he took advantage of, and so on. You need to actively search for these men who have been successful. They are out there, albeit in relatively small numbers. Try to engage new acquaintances in conversations that lend themselves to the lesbian transition. Of course, I have always been comfortable making that transition from most any topic. Let's say I am at a Halloween party and I see someone dressed as Wonder Woman. I lean over to the guy next to me and the language goes something like this:

"Hey, great costume over there, huh? I swear whenever I'd see Wonder Woman on TV with that magic lasso it would make me think that she's gotta be bisexual. No straight chick needs a lasso like that! So, does two chicks kissing turn you on?"

If the guy gives you a strange look and walks away, then he's probably a virgin and doesn't have any useful information for you anyway. It's better that he leaves now and free you up to talk to other knowledgeable men. Note that it doesn't matter what costume I see because it works for all of them. Suppose I see someone dressed as Snow White.

"Hey, do you think Snow White was a virgin? Cause all those horny dwarves must have laid into her at some point. What she really needed was a good woman to satisfy her. Am I right... huh?"

Suppose you are watching a football game at the local sports bar. There are always good-looking women in the beer commercials they air during football games. It might be appropriate to say something like,

"Hey, she'd look good in bed with my wife!"

At first you may be hesitant to say these things out loud. While this is normal, it is important to push through. The tone of your voice is just as important as the words you use. You want to sound confident that every man thinks Snow White was bisexual and that someone would have to be a moron to think otherwise. You don't want to come across as jokey or sarcastic. Those will not solicit the kinds of responses you need.

You can expect to hear from men the various ways that they have persuaded their significant others to sleep with women. You can get a wealth of information on specific scripts to use, how to set up a sexually conducive situation involving other women, and how to cope with the trade-offs that I mentioned earlier.

I would also recommend that you read magazines like *Penthouse Forum* and others that publish letters from readers. I know the authenticity of these letters is widely debated, but it really doesn't matter if they are true or not. A good idea is a good idea. There are also many websites and blogs devoted to sex and/or lesbian issues. These can be a great source of ideas.

I was at a Timberwolves game[16] in Minneapolis this one time and I got to talking with the guy sitting next to me. Like all polite, civilized people should, he asked me what I do. I told him I help people with their problems. He looks at me like I'm goofy, and he says, "You don't buy beer for kids, do you?" My Super Rope hit the floor. "No, Man, I help people get laid with two chicks at once." All of section 117 went completely silent. He says back to me, "I've done that!" Sections 116 and 118 were now noticeably quiet. "I've done that like four different times, man!"

That man's name was Chub Wilkins and this is his story:

---

[16] I got on Sportscenter that night. I was holding a sign that read, "Dan Patrick is my dad." I think it was February 1999. If anyone has a copy of that footage, contact me and we'll work out a trade.

"It was hot that day. In the jungle it's always hot. Charlie was in the brush just beyond the first ridge, and my rifle barrel was burning in anticipation. Stanley crawled up beside me. That boy had no concept of a man's need for space.

Stanley pulled out his dice. I grimaced, but only because I didn't want to give him the satisfaction of knowing that I was hooked. I pulled a few crumpled dollar bills from my fatigues. He rolled a five.

'Six the hard way,' I said.

The bastard threw a two and a four.

'Gimme odds on the five,' I said. Well, that son of a bitch rolled seven and I lost it. I threw down my weapon and started beating his ass."

"What the hell does this have to do with sleeping with two women at once?" I interrupted.

"He was sevening out after like two rolls all morning. I was setting the mood."

"What mood?"

"You didn't let me finish," he replied, "I was just getting to that."

"So the manager kicks me out of the paintball game for beating on Stanley, and that's when I ran into Lila in the parking lot. She was dressed to kill, but I was easy prey. Especially after I saw her kiss Samantha for luck.

'You don't want to go in there,' I warned them. 'Not before you loosen up first.'

"This was at a paintball facility?" I asked.

"That's right. I met my first wife there, too."

"Well, if you weren't in Vietnam then who the hell is Charlie?"

> When you work at a strip club, it's a job. The first week working there was awesome and the rest of the time it just sucked.

"That's Charlie coming up the stairs. He went to get some beers."

"Oh. Hey, Charlie, nice to meet you, man." I shook Charlie's hand and then turned back to Chub. "Man, this is a little far fetched. You meet some lesbians in the parking lot of a paintball facility and instead of going in and playing, they decide to have sex with you."

"I've also gotten laid at the Department of Motor Vehicles." He gnawed at a Super Rope.

"With two women at once?"

"No, but if the instructor had let my girlfriend ride along with us during the road test, then the answer might be different."

"Alright continue your story, and hey, that's been on the floor."

"So I says to Lila, 'Honey, I just spent fifty dollars that ain't getting refunded, and I still got a wad of paint that needs to be discharged. How about you and me and Miss Beauty Queen here go fire my gun?' To make a long story short, I spent the next hour in the back of their Chevy Blazer."

In conclusion, some stories are more entertaining than educational.

I have found the strip club scene to be a great spot to find people that can share their wisdom. I worked as a deejay at a club near my college back in the day. It was an extremely twisted experience that I never want to repeat but I'm glad I did it. Now, when I go to clubs, I am an insider and I can get all sorts of information from the people working there.

When you work at a strip club, it's a job. It's not at all like hanging out there. Your co-workers are hot women, true, but your co-workers also have inflated egos, often have friends and enemies amongst each other, and may try to use you as pawns in their moves against each other. God help you if you ever get to know the girls on a personal level. Most of them have more issues than Marvel Comics. Believe me, the first week working there was awesome and the rest of the time it just sucked.

This particular club encouraged the employees to drink on the job. We got our first two drinks free each night. After that, we had to pay $.50 a drink. It was common to have half a dozen drinks in a four hour shift, and often many more than that. The ladies got really pissy when they were drunk. They always wanted to have things exactly their way, and sometimes that wasn't possible. That was when I started using the phrase, "Sometimes, shit ain't fair, Princess." I would say that about twenty times a night.

Strippers fight about a lot of things, but one thing in particular is the songs they dance to. Most clubs will not let the same song be played by multiple strippers, so the ladies have to stake out the ones they want. A touring performer will get first pick, then it goes by seniority at the club. If another chick even picks a song by the same band as one of their songs, they can go ballistic on each other.

Occasionally, the strippers would proposition me. It was usually when they were drunk off their ass, and they were bored. More often than not, I would turn them down. I know that sounds hard to believe, but it just didn't seem worth the hassle most nights. Besides that, I really felt like I could nail the ones that were propositioning me anytime I wanted. Naturally, there were some ladies there I would have liked to spend time with, but they wouldn't make themselves available.

That little bit of information on being a strip club deejay should be enough for you to pretend to be a former deejay the next time you go to a club. In doing so, you become a member of a very select fraternity. You will be granted access to information by the bouncers, bartenders, deejays and disgusting washroom attendants. Use this status to chat with them about shit they have seen. You will be amazed.

The strippers[17] at the club may also have some good tips for you. Certainly, tell them you are a former deejay. They may see you as a safe guy because you worked with strippers before. Some guys want to make the jump to getting the strippers in bed. Let me just say, I have tried that and I think my wife shot the whole thing down just because the chick was a stripper. If she was a waitress, the night might have been fine, but all the wife heard was "stripper."

And before I end this chapter, I have to apologize to all my stripper friends out there. Not all strippers are annoying, immature and wallowing in self-loathing under their facade of physical beauty. Many of them are actually in medical school and just dancing to make their tuition and sponsor a little boy in Thailand who needs a well in his village. Wanna get a dance?

---

[17] Strippers prefer to be called dancers, so I call them dancers to their face. But they're strippers.

7: Make a Move

Remember when a game of ding-dong ditch was all we needed for a full day's worth of excitement? You'd run up to the house where the girl you liked lived, crouch down on the porch and look back at your friends hiding in the bushes across the street. Then you'd ring her doorbell only to take off running for those same bushes. From there you could watch in jubilation as her mother came to the door with a confused and then angry scowl on her face. Now we are so mature, or bored, or sick that we have to work out these elaborate plans that take years to implement, give rise to disastrous consequences, and yet they dominate our thought patterns.

In this chapter, I lay out several strategic maneuvers that you can adapt to your situation. I encourage you to use multiple maneuvers until you find one that works for you.

Pavlov's Dog

When I first got married, my wife and I were at this video store[18] and they had the "adults only" section behind the little curtain and she wouldn't go in. There was no one else in the store and we had just moved into town, so it wasn't like our neighbor was going to come around the corner with his kids and a copy of *The Fox and the Hound*. I couldn't get her in there to save my life. Now I can send her to the adult video store off the highway by herself and she knows which production companies shoot in HD, which stars work for which companies, and so on. Let me tell you how.

Pavlov was the guy with the dog and every time he fed the dog he would ring a bell just before putting the dish down. Well, the dog would salivate because he knew he was going to eat.

---

[18] For the younger generation, video stores are places people would go to get movies for their Video Cassette Recorder. It was a lot like a RedBox but big enough to walk inside and there was always a rude teenager working at the counter.

After a while Pavlov would only have to ring the bell and his dog would salivate even without the food. It is this concept, known as **conditional learning**, which we want to apply to our mission here.

Rent a porno with lots of chick on chick scenes.[19] You can usually tell from the title which ones they are. There are all kinds of female-only series out there, but all that really matters is that the chicks in the movie are hot. You don't want skanky dykes unless your mission is to develop your woman's attraction to skanky dykes. Next, think of something that you do to her that really excites her. Maybe it's eating her out, or maybe it's playing with her nipples a certain way. Just so long as it doesn't involve your dick, you're okay. Let's say for example that she likes her asshole fingered.

When the lesbo scenes come on screen, start her down that road to orgasm via asshole. Try and keep pace with the scene on the film so that your woman reaches her orgasm at the same time as the actresses in the film. Make sure she keeps looking at the screen while you are doing this to her. If she turns her head away to kiss you, suck you, or whatever, you stop the stimulus. Turn her head back towards the action and resume your stimulus. What we want is for her to associate her most heightened state of arousal with the sight or image of two women getting it on. Eventually, she will become aroused by the thought of two women ravaging one another. From there, it's possible she will be aroused by the thought of herself with another woman.

The number and consistency of pairings of the stimuli (the lesbo scenes and the orgasms) are responsible for the learning. If, however, you discontinue pleasuring her but you continue to show her the movies, she eventually will stop having the learned reaction orgasms. In other words, the effect will dissipate. For this reason, I encourage you to buy the annual subscription to your favorite pornsite rather than paying month to month.

To be fair, I think it is necessary to point out that a few actual psychology students I know[20] have hypothesized that one may

---

[19] See Appendix A: Girl on Girl Videos

[20] My friend Marcus is a student of life who once took a psychology course in college and now fancies himself some sort of expert.

experience what may be termed a "Lesbo Backlash," whereby the woman can *only* be aroused by another woman. This would leave you noticeably absent from the sexual equation. I'm not sure what the big deal is there. It sure beats a sharp stick in the eye. Like I said in the beginning of the book—you have to be flexible. If you get lemons, then you make lemonade.

Sidenote: Few people know that Pavlov's research was actually his own attempt at getting Mrs. Pavlov in the sack with his younger female assistant. His journal from the period prior to the beginning of the experiment with his dog confirmed this. Unfortunately, the journal, along with all other substantiating documents, were destroyed by the Nazis during World War II.

The Smart Mouse Gets the Cheese

Another form of training which we can exploit is called **instrumental learning**. Here, emphasis is placed on what the animal does and what kinds of outcomes follow its actions. In general, if a particular action is followed by an appreciated reward, the action will be repeated the next time the animal is in that same situation. It's the old experiment where the rat has to learn the maze in order to reach the cheese at the end. You run the maze over and over again until the rat has learned all the twists and turns necessary to complete the maze without getting lost.

Obviously, for our purposes, your woman is the rat, the maze is her journey towards bi-sexuality and the rewards are completely up to you. I think it's important to highlight the fact that the rewards need to be something the subject desires. If you plunked down two tickets to The Final Four, your college buddies might get excited, but she's probably not gonna care. I have included Appendix B at the back of the book which lists appropriate rewards.

The way I interpret it, you need to keep the rewards for specific behaviors uniform. For example, when she flirts with a woman she gets one thing. When she flirts with another woman, she gets an identical reward. When she asks a woman if she'd be interested in sleeping with you, she gets a different (perhaps greater) reward. If the rewards cease, then other behaviors will appear. Most learning situations involve some elements of both conditional and instrumental conditioning. Consider doing a combination of the two with your woman. Play the lesbo tape and get her excited to develop a response and then reward it with something you know she'll appreciate.

Something to keep in mind is what is referred to as the negatively accelerated learning curve. This is where the subjects show large gains at first, and then increasingly slower learning follows. This is similar to what I call the Blowjob Curve.

Based on my own experience and independent research[21], I have concluded that the first blowjob a man receives is the greatest, no matter how inexperienced the mouth is, simply because it is new and bizarre and incomprehensibly satisfying.

> Most learning situations involve some elements of both conditional and instrumental conditioning. Consider doing a combination of the two with your woman.

Unfortunately, the more you receive, the more the novelty of it wears off. It's sort of like riding the rollercoaster at your favorite amusement park. The first time is thrilling because you don't know where the twists and turns are or how long the ride will last. Each time thereafter, you pretty much know how it will go and it gets less and less thrilling. Still enjoyable, but not as good. If, however, you move to Swaziland where rollercoasters are harder to come by, you start to appreciate every chance you get to ride on one. As you get older, it's kind of like you moved to Swaziland because Mr. Johnson's encounters with the female mouth become much less frequent. Not only has it been a while since your last blowjob, but mentally you understand that it may be a long time until the next time, so you savor the sensation. At this point the level of satisfaction achieved during a blowjob

---

[21] I met these guys at a party in East Lansing, MI that shared my views and I think one of them was a biology major at MSU. At the very least he knew at lot about oral sex, and that's good enough for me.

increases, but never reaches the pleasure factor achieved during the first blowjob (See figure 3).

Based on the findings illustrated by the Blowjob Curve, I would recommend that you experiment with the rewards for a week or two and see how her behavior changes. Any worthwhile progress should be evident in that time. If progress appears minimal, I suggest you request a blowjob immediately and refer back to figure 3.

Figure 3.

Blowjob Curve

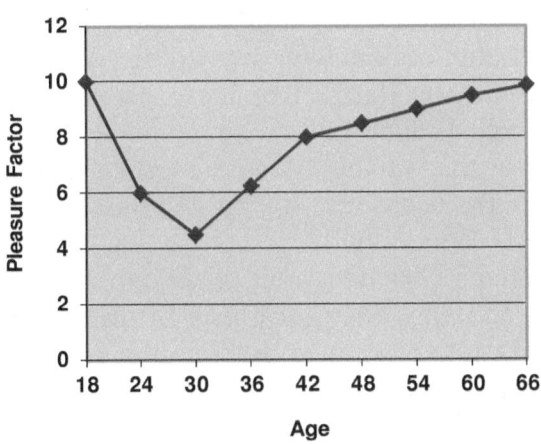

There is also the corresponding negatively accelerated curve of forgetting where the subject experiences large losses immediately after learning, then increasingly smaller losses. In order to retain what the subject has learned you must consistently review and repeat what you have taught. This means that if you slack off and don't keep up with your woman's training, it will all be wasted. If she must be constantly relearning that she has a sexual appetite for hot chicks, then she will never discover her true passion for sharing her lovers with you.

When in Rome...

This is where you create an atmosphere that is conducive to wild sexual activity. The idea is to get aquainted with other people that are into threesomes and start hanging out with them. Remember when you were in high school and your friends could convince you that just about the dumbest idea in the world was the greatest. It's the magic of peer pressure. Einstein said the eighth Wonder of the World was compound interest. He was wrong. It is peer pressure. Albert was a freak and he didn't have any friends, so he wouldn't really know. Why does it work? I haven't a fucking clue, but it does. How did your buddy convince you that your dad wouldn't realize you replaced his vodka with tap water? Some things defy comprehension.

Take your woman to parties that your new friends throw and let her mingle and get comfortable with everything. You want to introduce her to the various things that these people are into. Start buying lotions and beaded underwear. Maybe she won't like shag carpeting, but that's okay, because maybe she will like the new lava lamps in the bedroom. It's hit and miss; some will hit and some will miss. Hopefully the part about making out with the other women at the party will be a hit. I have to say that this is another one of those things that goes back to the frog in the boiling water thing. Don't spend an entire Saturday redecorating the house so that she shits a brick when she comes home.

On the more extreme (and desperate) side, you could plan a romantic getaway to the Mediterranean isle of Lesbos. Legend has it that in ancient times this chick poet, Sappho, was getting it on with fellow poet, Alcaeus, who was also devotedly attached to her female students. Tragically, like all Ancient Greeks, she killed herself because the Fates wouldn't stop fucking with her.[22] And she did it very dramatically by throwing herself off a cliff. This has led to the association of the island with female homosexuality and subsequently to the origination of the word lesbian. That's how I can be sure that the stories must be true.

---

[22] She did it over some sailor who probably wouldn't have appreciated her anyway. It was quite sad.

The Forbidden Fruit

This is so asinine that I can't even believe I'm mentioning it, but I know guys who try this. They essentially use reverse psychology on their women to try and increase their desire for the opposite sex. Supposedly, if they make it seem like they don't want them to sleep with chicks and they forbid them from sleeping with chicks, their wives are going to want it. The thing is, that only works on five-year olds. If your wife is that dumb, then why do you need this book? Because we are the idiots!

If you tell her that she cannot sleep with other women and you are definitely not going to sleep with other women, then she is just going to shrug and say okay. It's one less bullshit hang-up of yours that she has to put up with. Obviously, this is one of the strategies that I would not recommend, because unlike the others, it's simply implausible. Skip it.

Paying Strangers to Help

If you ever get the chance to see the film *Can't Buy Me Love* with Patrick Dempsey, I highly recommend it. Dempsey's character in the film has an interesting theory. He is this hopeless nerd who wants to be popular, so he offers to pay the most popular girl in school $1,000 to go out with him for one month. This, he theorizes, will positively affect the way the rest of the high school population perceives him. Of course, it works for a while but then backfires and yada yada yada. My theory is that we can use that same tactic of paying people for behaviors beneficial to the cause in order to positively affect the way our women perceive us.

Suppose that a very attractive woman on your payroll approaches your wife and tells her quite frankly that she thinks she is gorgeous and would like to take her to a hotel. Hopefully, she is flattered. Without a doubt she will have a reaction. If exposed to such incidents for a prolonged period of time I see this going in one of two directions. First, she could develop a homophobic complex that manifests itself in the form of bedwetting and an anxiety disorder. The second possibility I see is a surrender of her soul to the whims of the hordes of women who want to play games with her body.

I think it's important to point out that neither scenario is desirable.[23]   You want your dart to land somewhere in the middle, so best not to spend too much on chicks hitting on your woman. Spread 'em out over a period of time, and don't give them the same thing to say to her. A friend of mine would give the girls a script to use and they would basically commit the thing to memory. His wife was in a Cracker Barrel and this woman said word for word what a different woman had said to her at Wal-mart ten days earlier. So let me also say that this is not a tactic that can accomplish the mission on its own. It must be part of a much larger and more diverse plan.

More directly related to the movie I mentioned, you could pay someone to make you look more attractive to your wife and/or potential threesome participants. If you think you need to pay someone to pretend to be attracted to you in order to convince your wife that she should be having sex with you, then I recommend you read the book, <u>Leaving the Frigid Woman Behind</u> by Lee Verpore and <u>Life's Too Short to Stay with That Bitch</u> by J.T. Bangmuff. If you want to pay a chick to flirt with you in order to persuade a third woman to join you, then hopefully you already have the approval of your woman. Good luck trying to explain to your wife that you paid a woman to flirt with you in order to attract this other woman, but you never really wanted to do anything with the one that you paid. As you say that out loud, imagine the look on her face as she listens to you. You're screwed.

Hypnosis

I don't understand hypnosis at all. Every time I have seen it done in movies or the few times I have seen it live on stage, it looks completely phony. I always think it must be an illusion and I just can't figure out the magician's trick. But, I have to admit that <u>I have been hypnotized</u>.

---

[23] The soul surrender thing would be my preference if I absolutely had to choose, but it seems a bit over the top.

I used to work for a very large corporation and I was attending the annual Christmas party. The company had arranged for a hypnotist to entertain us after dinner. The hypnotist called for volunteers and, of course, no one raised their hand. I was drafted.

I got on stage with about four or five of my co-workers and I remember the hypnotist asking us to close our eyes and concentrate on his voice. Nothing he said gave me the impression that he was trying to hypnotize me. I felt awake and alert the whole time I was up there. He asked us to raise our hands if we felt him touching us with a feather, and I felt it, so I raised my hand. I heard the crowd roar with laughter.

> Hypnosis is used for all sorts of things... How can we subvert this technique for our own sexual gratification?

A few minutes later, I opened my eyes and walked off the stage. My eyes met those of one of my co-workers and he exclaimed, "That guy never touched you once!"

Those at my dinner table informed me that I was up there for fifteen minutes and did everything the hypnotist told me to do, some of which I could not recall. I was convinced he had touched me with a feather, but they assured me that the hypnotist did not even have a feather.

How could this be? I have no idea.

Hypnosis is used for all sorts of things including, smoking cessation programs, weight loss, sleep disorders and pain management. Up until that night, I thought it was all crap. But I believe that somehow it must work—at least for some people. Now the question becomes, how can we subvert this technique for our own sexual gratification?

I have checked out books at the library, staked out hypnotists' dressing rooms, and even taken up smoking so that I could try the smoking cessation hypnosis program, but I haven't figured out a way to hypnotize my wife.

Nevertheless, I remain convinced that it can be done, and I encourage anyone to get educated or find a mentor. That said, I believe it is a bad idea to pay a trained hypnotist to hypnotize your wife for you. Once he has her under his control, he could do anything to her. He's obviously unscrupulous or he wouldn't be helping you. There's nothing to stop him from hypnotizing you either. In the snap of his fingers he'll have your wife on his dick and you'll be his helper monkey.

The Spokesman

When you break it all down, what we really need is to change your woman's attitude towards sleeping with chicks. Social psychologists have conducted studies on how and why people change their attitudes and they have come up with the **balance theory**. If, for example, your woman hears a speech from someone who she holds in high regard, she will typically expect to hear ideas with which she agrees. If that is not the case, then either she will like the speaker less, or she will adjust her attitude and like the ideas more. Thus, your woman will bring her attitudes toward the speaker and the ideas into balance. Similarly, people tend to try to balance, or reconcile, their own ideas with their actions.

The discovery that attitudes follow from behavior as well as vice versa emerges from the well-tested assumption that people desire to preserve logical consistency in their views of themselves and their environments. A number of theories of cognitive consistency have become important in social psychological thinking. These theories stress the idea that individuals need to believe that their own thoughts and actions are in agreement with one another, and that perceiving inconsistency between one's actions and thoughts leads to attempts to reduce that inconsistency. To sum it up, your woman doesn't like chicks, but if someone she respects or admires thinks two women having sex is cool, then she will need to re-evaluate her respect for that individual or her decision to not pursue her own female lover.

What you need to do is find someone that she respects or admires and convince them to help you. That can be tricky. Any women that you know are liable to rat you out. I'm not saying that women in general are not trustworthy. It just seems like they focus too much on the fact that someone admires them rather than looking at the big picture. You can try and give this chick the old story about the soldier jumping onto the grenade to save the general or laying down a bunt to advance the tying run to second base, but it's like talking to a brick wall. Women have no sense of these things. I highly recommend that you not put your faith in another woman working with you on this.

A man, on the other hand, will certainly be more likely to help you. I can't think of one man I know that wouldn't sacrifice his integrity for a shot at a threesome. But that is just the problem with men. You run the risk of that man wanting in on your woman's action. That may or may not be cool with you, but you should be ready for that possibility.

The best way to approach this is to keep everything under your control. With today's desktop publishing software and high quality printers you can print up a fake newspaper with an article about your woman's idol. Don't recreate a local paper. That is too easy for to recognize as being phony. Try for a national tabloid or something, but again, don't copy an existing one. If you show her an article from your *National Enquirer* she can easily go to her friend's copy of that issue and see that it doesn't match. Then you've got some explaining to do.

A friend and I worked jointly on this project for use on our wives last year. We created a December 2010 issue of *Gentleman's Monthly*, which featured an interview with John Travolta and Kelly Preston. Both of our wives think John Travolta is hot and makes great movies and blah, blah, blah. I believe we exploited that admiration expertly. *(Note to John: If you are reading this- thanks for taking one for the team.)*

Gentleman's Monthly
December 2010
Written by Captain Robert Morgan

I recently had the pleasure of sitting down with two of Hollywood's biggest stars in the living room of their California home. It was a break in the action for both of them, and they were enjoying spending time alone with their newborn baby. I was not the least bit sorry for having interrupted them.

Captain: John, I just watched *Pulp Fiction* for the hundredth time and man is that shit funny!

John: Thanks. I worked real hard on that character and thankfully all of the other cast and crew members were excellent. We were able to make a great picture.

CRM: I wonder though if it wouldn't have been better if we had seen Uma Thurman naked?

JT: Yeah, maybe. She may have been nude in some of her earlier films.

CRM: You're kidding. Do you have a list handy?

JT: No, I really don't keep track of...

CRM: No, I shouldn't have put you on the spot like that in front of the Mrs. Anyway, how are things with you, Kelly?

Kelly: Great! I'm starting work on my next film in a couple of weeks. It's called...

CRM: No. No, I mean how are things with you *sexually*?

KP: Excuse me? What was your name again? I don't think I know you well enough for you to be asking me such a question.

CRM: John, back me up here, buddy.

JT: Kelly, I think that Robert just wants to get a feel for how we are doing as a couple in the sexual arena. It's a valid question given the fact that we are celebrities and we have forfeited our right to privacy.

KP: Alright, Johnny Bear, but if I get all horny from the love talk we'll have to cut this interview short and make Robert here baby-sit for an hour or two.

CRM: Atta girl, Kelly.

KP: Well, things are pretty good in that regard, too. John was kind enough to share a secret with me recently that has really helped open my eyes to a wider range of sexual pleasures.

CRM: Well, I'm dying to know what that was.

KP: John has apparently been attracted to one of my best friends for a number of years, but he was afraid to tell me about it.

CRM: You're kidding. Why is that, John?

JT: Captain, it's just that people today are so close-minded. Now, I'm grateful that my wife isn't that way, but it was just difficult for me to get past the fear that I might be rejected, or that my beautiful wife might somehow misinterpret my feelings as love for this other woman. It wasn't about love.

CRM: Of course it wasn't.

JT: It was just that I was attracted to this other woman, something totally beyond my control. The fact that it was someone that Kelly is friends with made it more difficult because I would see her on a regular basis.

KP: John told me about it, and I was hurt at first. I didn't understand how he could love me and still lust after someone else. I didn't realize that a man could lust after many women at once while still retaining love and loyalty to one.

CRM: That's dynamite. What happened after John revealed his secret.

JT: We called her friend right away and told her the whole story and it turns out that she was attracted to me as well.

KP: She was afraid to tell me because she wasn't sure how I'd react. Once we were all comfortable with the fact that this kind of thing was normal, we decided to go for it.

CRM: You mean you all had sex together?

(They are smiling at each other and making goo goo eyes.)

CRM: Any chance that I might get some details, photos, ringside seat at the next event?

JT: That's doubtful, Captain.

CRM: Well, I'd love to baby-sit now if you two have something you'd rather be doing.

KP: You're on!

Phonetics

I saw this movie with Sandra Bullock from like 1978, and it was called *Love Potion #9*. It was about this social misfit who was a biochemist. Well, he goes to this palm reader and she gives him this potion, love potion #8, actually. This potion makes whoever drinks it irresistible to the opposite sex and abhorrent to members of the same sex. The nerdy guy took it back to his lab and discovered that the potion stimulated tiny hairs in his throat and changed the sound of his voice ever so slightly. Understanding that not everything that comes out of

71

Hollywood is factual, I had to check out any factual basis behind the screenwriter's idea.

It turns out that there is an entire science devoted to determining how the human ear perceives the sounds of speech. I'm not talking about fictitious hairs in your throat either. I'm talking about things in your woman's brain that trigger positive and negative reactions, the way she perceived your tone of voice, and all the other things that make up a woman's intuition. It brings to mind the widely held belief that chicks dig guys with accents.

But chicks don't dig every accent they hear. There are some accents that chicks dig deeper than others and some not at all. When a woman from Topeka is greeted by a guy from Oklahoma City, she sees him as just an average guy. That same Topekan female when approached by a guy from France will be aroused by his voice. The mysterious stranger will only have to speak to her in his native tongue in order to lure her like a vengeful sailor preying on the muted siren of mythical lore. Or something like that.

To further test my theory, my team of researchers worked around the clock to study the effects of various accents on the female species[24]. The results of which are fascinating to say the least. We asked our respondents to classify each accent as sexy, favorable, unfavorable or repulsive. What follows is a breakdown how the various accents scored in our research.

Sexy	Favorable	Unfavorable	Repulsive
Boston	French	Mississippi Southern	Indian
Australian	English	Canadian	Oriental
Irish	Latin American	Pirate	German
Russian Fermale	Jamacian	Russian Male	

Obviously, it is to your advantage to master the accents which scored well in our survey. I have found that the best way to

---

[24] My team consisted of myself, my buddy Sean and a concessionist at Six Flags Great America. They charge $4.25 for a sno-cone!

> The mysterious stranger will only have to speak to her in his native tongue in order to lure her like a vengeful sailor preying on the muted siren of mythical lore.

develop an accent is to mimic someone else. Again, studying film is a great way to go. Watch the movies *Good Will Hunting, Crocodile Dundee* and *Far and Away* and you'll be set. I'd also be remiss if I didn't draw your attention to the fact that the ladies really seemed to like the Russian accent on a woman. This leads me to believe that we might have a better shot at the threesome if we promised to have a Russian chick in the fray. Way sorry to those guys whose native tongues were rated repulsive. Don't shoot the messenger, eh? And I was really surprised about the pirate rating. That's been my signature for like three years.

"Aargh, would you like to go out on me barge and help me hoist the mailsail?"

Alcohol

Alcohol, in my opinion, is the single most effective way to get your woman to sleep with chicks. It is not, however, a good place to start your mission.

Alcohol is the <u>closer</u>.

Throughout this book I have talked about using language to set the stage for the waitress and the soccer moms. I have suggested how to weed out undesirable prospects. I have suggested psychological techniques. Once you have brought your wife and the female prospect to the brink of the ménage a trois, offer them some drinks.

Alcohol lowers inhibitions, affects the drinker's judgment, can increase sexual arousal and limit self-control. That's pretty much everything you want to have happen to your wife and the prospect in this situation.

Have alcohol ready at home. Stock a liquor cabinet with all the staples: vodka, rum, tequila, whiskey, gin, red wine, white wine, and a few different beers. If you don't have a good blender, invest in one. Have lemons, limes, olives and maraschino cherries on hand. Get a how-to video on bartending so you can mix up some fun drinks when the ladies come over. Watch the movie Cocktail and practice throwing bottles around. Make drinking at your place the best time a gal could have.

Once you have the women home, offer them drinks. If they don't want them, don't force it, but fix yourself one. Make it a weak drink so you don't get too far ahead of them. The last thing you want is to get sloppy and lose your edge. You need to stay sharp in order to make the final move.

Are there consequences to using alcohol? Sure. They may feel the sting of regret in the morning. Who among us can't relate? But so long as you didn't force the alcohol on them, you're not to blame for their actions. Of course, they may not see it that way...

If you get your wife drunk and the threesome goes down, she may accuse you of being manipulative. I swear that I have found it's always easier to ask for forgiveness than it is to ask for permission. So if the wife is going to be pissed, say you're sorry and hope she gets over it. If she can't get over it, at least you had your fun. She can't ever take that away from you. I guess the downside is that you're unlikely to have another threesome with her.

Getting the other woman drunk, on the other hand, does not bring with it nearly the same amount of consequences as getting your woman drunk. If the chick you are with is a relative stranger and she gets upset about what happened, who gives a shit? So long as you didn't force anything on her, what she thinks the morning after should mean about as much to you as the score of last year's Music City Blowjob Bowl brought to you by Frito's.

Pull the Trigger

When the threesome is imminent, it's time to prepare. Depending on your age, that might mean heading to the pharmacy for some ED pills.[25] For the rest of us, let's run down a list of chores.

1. **Clean the house.** Pine Sol that motherfucker to get the floors spotless, rugs stain-free, and all the smells out of the upholstery. No one wants to get naked in a place where they wonder what the hell smells so bad.
2. **Ditch the kids.** If you have kids, send them to grandma's house. If you have a sitter who comes to your place, give her the keys to your minivan and have her drive around the block 900 times.
3. **Board the pets.** Some people don't like animals. If your third is one of those people and she is uncomfortable, it's going to ruin the mood. Don't let it kill the deal.
4. **Go shopping.** You need alcohol to close the deal, condoms to fuck the strange, and maybe some fresh porn to ease into it.
5. **Think about hygiene.** While you are at the store, you might pick up some extra toothbrushes. The chick is going to want to brush her teeth once you're done with her. Maybe even spring for some mouthwash. She might also need some baby wipes. It depends on how kinky you are.
6. **Do laundry.** Before it starts, the ladies will appreciate clean sheets. When it's over, you'll all want to shower, so be ready with some clean towels.

There will come a point when you have to take a leap. You will have done everything you can do to tee it up, stack the odds in your favor, and then you have to pull the trigger.

---

[25] Realistically, you might be more likely to score with two women at once when you're older. Many of your male competitors will have died of heart disease and cancer. The women they leave behind are desperate to find someone so they don't die alone. Even a creepy old bastard with sick fantasies starts looking pretty attractive.

Accept the fact that your wife is not going to come out and propose the threesome. She is not going to initiate it with the other woman. You will have to make that first move.

I can't tell you how to psyche yourself up for it. We all have our own way. Before my first time, I excused myself to the bathroom and I listened to the song from Rocky II that starts right when Adrian whispers to him from the hospital bed, "Win. Win." I heard those horns and I knew what I had to do. I was going to eat lightning and crap thunder.

Go out there and kiss the woman. Say it out loud, that you want to see them kiss. Press their mouths together. Get it started.

8: Believe it Can Happen

Believing that one day you will be having sex with your wife and another woman can generate enough positive energy to light Yankee Stadium for nine innings. Believing that one day your wife will come home and ask you if you would like to invite her best friend over for a game of strip poker can add several good years to your pack-a-day-smoking-bacon-and-egg-eating-no-exercise-except-to-reach-for-your-remote-control life. Just the thought of it is enough joy to get you through the toughest of days. Even if it never materializes, they can never take that joy away from you.

My friend Craig was telling me about an experiment with **learned helplessness**. What these scientists did was get some dogs and put them in a room where the floor was electrified in some areas. The dogs would bark and yelp when they would get electrocuted, because it hurts, you know. Eventually, the dogs figured out where the safe spots were and they would lie down there. Then they put some dogs in a room where the floor was completely electrified. The dogs walked around for a while trying to find a safe spot until they finally laid down. They were being electrocuted, but they learned that there was nothing they could do to avoid the shocks. They just gave up searching.

We men are very similar to those dogs in our attitude towards our wives and sex. We have searched for women that were into it. We have tried asking them in a variety of ways only to be met with hostility. We have laid down on the electric floor and we accept the pain that it inflicts on us. The only difference between us and the dogs is that we do not live on a fully electric floor. There are safe spots. There are opportunities for sex with multiple women. There are men living the dream. You need to get up off the electric floor and continue to search for those safe spots.

You need to have a positive attitude. Your wife will pick up on this and it will help you. Anyone in sales will tell you that in order to sell something you have to be enthusiastic about it.

Think back to the last time you bought a car, and imagine the salesman's dialogue like this:

Salesman: *"So, this car here has leather seats, of course, with your kids they will probably tear the damn things up and it'll look like shit in a couple weeks. Your kids look like rambunctious little bastards; maybe it'll only take 'em ten days. The stereo is great, but for the money you'll be paying it ain't worth it, besides when they come out with the next great sound technology in the next ten minutes you'll have to rip that sucker out 'cause it ain't upgradable. Now that I think about it though, you look a little too old to appreciate a decent sound system anyway."*

You wouldn't buy the car, and after kicking in the guy's teeth you'd probably be soured on the idea of a new car altogether. That is the kind of effect that you can have on your woman. If you have a smile on your face and a bounce in your step every time you make a move towards your goal, she will pick up on that positive energy.

> We have laid down on the electric floor and we accept the pain that it inflicts on us.

You need to stay positive because it will also help you stay the course. All the bullshit and rejection and failure is something that will test you and it will be easy to become disillusioned. If you allow that to happen you may decide to abandon your goal. Don't let this happen. Believing that you can do it will keep you positive and keep you in the game.

Not that I believe in it, per se, but we need all the help we can get, and in these trying times, I suggest you look at your karma. Karma is the Hindu name for their morality scorecard. *(No offense to Hindus intended, but I have to simplify this admittedly complex concept. This is a sex guide, not a religion text).*

It goes like this: If you help an old lady with her grocery cart you get some good karma. If you hit a dog with your car, you get some bad karma. The idea is to accumulate as much good karma as possible without inconveniencing yourself too much. The people with the best karma at the end of their life get reincarnated as those lucky bastards that have hot looking lesbians falling in their lap. The guys with shitty karma come back as tapeworms or bed bugs.

Maybe being good in this life will only help you in the next one and has nothing to do with the here and now, but at least it's something. Maybe Santa Claus is real and like the song says, he's watching us to see if we are naughty or nice. Maybe there is a wealthy philanthropist living in your town searching for a do-gooder to shower with the money and power it takes to lure the gold-diggers. There's nothing wrong with a little recognition. Maybe Michael Landon didn't really die, and he's wandering the country as a real life angel hooking people up. Maybe you shop at the same Wal-Mart as Hugh Hefner. Maybe if you help the guy out with his groceries he'll toss a little Playmate action your way. I'm not saying he'll give you one of the current models, but maybe one of the older, washed up ones that is still hanging around the mansion that he can't seem to shake. You can catch more chicks with honey than you can with vinegar.

I thought I would close with a few statistics that will no doubt instill in you the confidence that you can succeed.[26]

- 90% of men say they have gotten a less than violent response from their partner after disclosing their desire to include another woman in their sex life
- 50% of men claim to have been with two women at once
- The other 50% didn't understand the question, and might possibly have made the same claim had I surveyed them before their last beer
- 40% of women wouldn't leave their boyfriends simply for making a request for a threesome
- 80% of those that said they wouldn't leave their boyfriends say that they would be too lazy to find some other jerk who would probably just want to do the same thing but be too big of a wimp to say anything about it

---

[26] Statistics based on a survey conducted at that same party in East Lansing.

Kinda makes you think we're making some progress, huh?

Appendix A: Girl on Girl Videos

- Wet Lesbians Weekend
- When the Boys Are Away the Girls Will Play
- Girls Just Want to Have Fun
- Lez Be Friends
- Holla Black Girlz
- Chick Flick
- Two Chicks No Dicks
- Dirty Dykes
- Smoking in the Girls Room
- Where the Boys Aren't
- Dyke Hard
- Girly Thoughts
- Strap-on MILF Hookers
- Lesbo Finger Poppers
- Sorority Splash
- Lesbian Love Slaves
- Strap-on Club
- Home Schooled
- Lesbian Heaven
- Decadent Divas

Appendix B: Things Chicks Dig

- Tickets to a Bon Jovi concert
- Those shower attachments that let you change the water stream from real hard to gentle
- Blackjack gum
- Flowers[27]
- Play with her hair (free!)
- Lotions that smell like cucumber and watermelon and posies
- Original limericks- steal some from The Beatles, Whitesnake or Justin Timberlake depending on her age
- Epsom salts
- Buy one, get one free bungie jumping
- A night at a swanky hotel
- The naked station at aforementioned swanky hotel
- A Swedish massage
- Cash
- Fun size Snickers
- Pom-poms
- Mail order seeds

---

[27] See previous comment regarding gas station flowers

Appendix C: What Book Are You Reading?

For all of the slow-witted readers who will be stumped when their wives ask them what they are reading, I have added Appendix C. None of these responses should warrant follow-up questions or conversation as they are ridiculously dull. But just in case, I threw in some quick reference points.

- Famous Monkeys of the 19th Century (Kiki, J.P. the Apey, Hansel the Danish orangutan)
- TechWeek's Annual Top 100 Sparkplug Distributors issue (4M, Midwest Sparks)
- Milwaukee Metalfest Band Spotlight (Desecration, Crutch Bucket, Grave Images)
- Pollens of North America (Mexico, Canada, United States)
- The Bowler's Dictionary (strike, spare, split)
- Foot Odor Prevention: A Chronological History (Dr. William Scholl began selling foot products in 1906!)
- Famous Tunnels of Europe (Laerdal Tunnel in Norway)
- Tales of Tortured and Misunderstood Bible Villians (Goliath, Judas, Pharoah)
- Laughter or Yak Milk: Nepal's Prescription for Healthy Shirpas

I also thought it might be helpful for you to be ready with some answers if your woman overhears you mentioning the book with someone. Please note that the inclusion of this section does not in any way condone the open discussion of or allusion to this book. Remember: Venus has spies everywhere! If she hears you say the book title, teel her she misheard you. What you really said was:

How to Get Your Knife to Do Tricks
How to Get a Tent to Sleep Six
A Day in the Life of Cheap Trick

Remember the bullshitter's secret: Say it quickly and with confidence and it sounds like the truth.